FAMILY LIFE
HomeBuilders
COUPLES SERIES®

BUILDING

YOUR

MARRIAGE

BIBLE STUDY ELECTIVE

DENNIS RAINEY

Gospel Light

How to Let the Lord Build Your House *and not labor in vain.*

FamilyLife is a division of Campus Crusade for Christ Incorporated, an evangelical Christian organization founded in 1951 by Bill Bright. FamilyLife was started in 1976 to help fulfill the Great Commission by strengthening marriages and families and then equipping them to go to the world with the gospel of Jesus Christ. Our FamilyLife Marriage Conference is held in most cities throughout the United States and is one of the fastest-growing marriage conferences in America today. Information on all resources offered by FamilyLife may be obtained by either writing or calling us at the address and telephone number listed below.

Publishing Staff

William T. Greig, Publisher

Dr. Elmer L. Towns, Senior Consulting Publisher

Dr. Gary S. Greig, Senior Consulting Editor

Jean Daly, Managing Editor

Pam Weston, Editorial Assistant

Kyle Duncan, Editorial Director

Bayard Taylor, M.Div., Editor, Theological and Biblical Issues

Building Your Marriage Bible Study Elective

ISBN 0-8307-1812-5

Dennis Rainey, Executive Director
FamilyLife
P.O. Box 23840
Little Rock, AR 72221-3840
(501) 223-8663
A Division of Campus Crusade for Christ Incorporated
Bill Bright, Founder and President
Published by Gospel Light, Ventura, California 93006

How to Make Clean Copies from This Book

You may make copies of portions of this book with a clean conscience if:

- you (or someone in your organization) are the original purchaser;
- you are using the copies you make for a noncommercial purpose (such as teaching or promoting your ministry) within your church or organization;
- you follow the instructions provided in this book.

However, it is ILLEGAL for you to make copies if:

- you are using the material to promote, advertise or sell a product or service other than for ministry fund-raising;
- you are using the material in or on a product for sale;
- you or your organization are **not** the original purchaser of this book.

By following these guidelines you help us keep our products affordable.

Thank you,

Gospel Light

To Jerry and Sheryl Wunder,
because your friendship, servanthood and lives
have made **The HomeBuilders Couples Series®** a reality.

SESSION 1:

Overcoming Isolation: Identifying the Problem 29
Selfishness and isolation are the major obstacles to building oneness and a
godly marriage.

SESSION 2:

Overcoming Isolation: Defeating the Problem 45
Defeating selfishness and isolation is essential in building oneness and a
godly marriage.

SESSION 3:

Creating Oneness: Benefits and Principles 57
Oneness in marriage brings rich benefits to a couple as they both pursue
unity instead of selfishly putting individual interests first.

SESSION 4:

Creating Oneness: God's Purpose for Marriage 71
Oneness in marriage is achieved as both husband and wife yield to God
and work together in building their home from the same set of blueprints:
the Bible.

SESSION 5:

Receiving Your Mate: Recognizing Your Need 81
Oneness in marriage requires receiving your mate as God's perfect
provision for your needs.

SESSION 6:

Receiving Your Mate: God's Perfect Provision 91
Oneness in marriage requires receiving your mate, regardless of his or her
imperfections, as God's perfect provision for your needs.

SESSION 7:

Constructing a Relationship: Leave and Cleave .103
The process of becoming one requires that a couple construct their marriage
by leaving parents and cleaving to each other.

SESSION 8:

Constructing a Relationship: Becoming One Flesh 115
The process of becoming one requires that a couple construct their marriage
by leaving parents, cleaving to each other and becoming one flesh.

SESSION 9 HUSBANDS:

Fitting Together Part One 125
There are three biblical responsibilities God wants a husband to assume
toward his wife: servant-leadership, unselfish loving and caring.

ACKNOWLEDGMENTS

The following Bible study is a result of the vision and labor of a team of individuals committed to strengthening marriages around the world. While I owe many thanks to the entire FamilyLife staff, a few "heroes" deserve special recognition.

First, my friend and colleague Jerry Wunder has been, in many ways, the heart behind this entire project. His unwavering belief in this study has endured months of writing, testing and final reworking.

Bob Horner played an instrumental role throughout this process through his vital conceptual and content advice. Robert Lewis, Bill McKenzie and Lee Burrell also made significant contributions toward the content of the Bible study. For help during its earliest stages, I must also thank Mark Dawson and Mike Rutter.

As the study neared completion, a few of our staff emerged as true "champions of the cause." First, there is Julie Denker, whose writer's touch added clarity and definition to my periodic ramblings! And then there are Jeff Lord, who served faithfully as my researcher, and Fred Hitchcock with his indispensable editing abilities. And finally, there is Donna Guirard and her finishing touches on the "look" and design of the series.

Julie and Jeff also spent many hours at the word processor entering seemingly endless revisions. As always, Jeff Tikson pitched in, especially when I became ill, and pushed the study through to the end.

Don and Sally Meredith have also influenced our ministry and our lives in so many ways and, as a result, leave a legacy through this study.

There were many groups—around the country—who participated in pilot home studies. Thanks for your feedback. It was invaluable.

I need to extend a heartfelt word of appreciation to Wes Haystead. Thank you, Wes, for coming alongside our team and helping to make this dream a reality.

And last, to Dave Boehi, I say thanks to God because you have been a real difference maker in tens of thousands of marriages through **The HomeBuilders Couples Series®**. I'm privileged to have worked with you over the past decade!

INTRODUCTION

About The HomeBuilders Couples Series®

What is the purpose of the HomeBuilders Series?

Do you remember the first time you fell in love? That junior high—or elementary school—"crush" stirred your affections with little or no effort on your part. We use the term "falling in love" to describe the phenomenon of suddenly discovering our emotions have been captured by someone delightful.

Unfortunately, our society tends to make us think that all loving relationships should be equally effortless. Thus millions of couples, Christians included, approach their marriages certain that the emotions they feel will carry them through any difficulties. And millions of couples quickly learn that a good marriage does not automatically happen.

Otherwise intelligent people, who would not think of buying a car, investing money, or even going to the grocery store without some initial planning, enter into marriage with no plan of how to make their marriage succeed.

But God has already provided the plan, a set of blueprints for a truly godly marriage. His plan is designed to enable two people to grow together in a mutually satisfying relationship, and then to look beyond their own marriage to others. Ignoring this plan leads to isolation and separation between husband and wife—the pattern so evident in the majority of homes today. Even when great energy is expended, failure to follow God's blueprints results in wasted effort, bitter disappointment—and, in far too many cases, divorce.

In response to this need in marriages today, FamilyLife of Campus Crusade for Christ created a popular series of small-group Bible studies for couples called **The HomeBuilders Couples Series®**. The series has now been adapted for larger groups such as adult Sunday School classes. Now you can lead a class of adults in a study designed to answer one question for couples:

How do you build a distinctively Christian marriage?

It is our hope that in answering this question with the biblical blueprints for building a home, we will see the development of growing, thriving marriages filled with the love of Jesus Christ.

FamilyLife is committed to strengthening your family. We hope **The HomeBuilders Couples Series®** will assist you and your church as it equips couples in building godly homes.

What is this study intended to accomplish?

Couples who participate in these sessions will find that the experience:

- Stimulates them to examine what Scripture says about how to construct a solid, satisfying marriage.
- Allows them to interact with each other on a regular basis about significant issues in their marriages.
- Encourages them to interact with other couples, establishing mutual accountability for growth efforts.
- Motivates them to take specific actions which have been valuable to couples desiring to build stronger homes.
- Creates accountability to others for growth in their marriages.

Why is accountability so important?

Accountability is a scriptural principle that tells us to "be subject to one another in the fear of Christ" (Ephesians 5:21). This means I choose to submit my life to the scrutiny of another person in order to gain spiritual strength, growth and balance.

Accountability means asking another person for advice. It means giving him or her the freedom to make honest observations and evaluations about you. It means you're teachable and approachable. True accountability involves letting another person into the interior of your life.

Adult classes which use a HomeBuilders Couples study are opening themselves up for at least a small measure of accountability. Our experience has shown that many class members will make commitments to apply aspects of the studies to their lives, but will never follow through on those commitments. As a leader, establishing an environment of friendly accountability can help your class members get the most out of this study.

Look for some hints on establishing accountability in the "Tips for Leading Your Class" section.

What impact has The HomeBuilders Couples Series® had in marriages?

Since we published the first HomeBuilders study in 1987, we've continually heard stories about couples whose marriages were revitalized and, in some cases, even saved. Here are some examples:

"We started our HomeBuilders group as a follow-up to the Video FamilyLife Conference presented at our church. We have developed a good openness among the group members. It has brought problem areas to the surface and given us a greater sense of awareness of our responsibility toward our mate. One couple travels as far as an hour to attend!"

Pastor, Washington

"We're using Building Your Marriage and Mastering Your Money in Marriage in our Sunday school classes, both for newlyweds and as a marriage renewal class. I have seen couples open communication lines for the first time in a long time as a result of their involvement."

Bill Willits
Minister to Married Adults
First Baptist Church
Atlanta, Ga.

"We've led three studies now, and in each one of those we have seen ourselves grow. You really do co-learn."

Doug Grimm
Playa Del Rey, Calif.

"I've built my family ministry around the FamilyLife Conference and the HomeBuilders. It makes biblically-minded, servant-minded people who are useful for advancing the kingdom and leadership of the kingdom."

Jeff Rhodes, pastor
First Presbyterian Church
Winterhaven, Fla.

"Nine weeks of the HomeBuilders class turned everything around in our relationship. It was a real miracle. The walls came down and the masks came off. We were able to discuss matters we had swept under the carpet years ago that our enemy was consistently using to destroy the love God had designed for us since the beginning of time....

"The HomeBuilders class really works. Here is why: HomeBuilders not only shows you why, and tells you how, it teaches a way to alter your life-style so these great truths become a part of everyday living.

"We have truly overcome isolation and are building toward oneness in our marriage. We have learned how to yield to God and the leading of His Holy Spirit instead of our own selfish desires...the romance is back and the intimacy is growing every day. HomeBuilders has really given us the 'wisdom' we were looking for in our marriage.

"It is absolutely the best thing that has ever happened to us since becoming Christians 18 years ago. It changed our lives at a time I was just ready to accept apathy for parts of my marriage, figuring there was no way to ever change."

Alan and Lanette Hauge
Playa Del Rey, Calif.

How does this study fit into a strategy for building Christian marriages?

While this study has great value in itself, it is only the first step in a long-term process of growth. If people complete these sessions and then gradually return to their previous patterns of living, little or no good will result. Continued effort is required for people to initiate and maintain new directions in their marriages.

It is our belief, also, that no couple can truly build a Christian home and marriage without a strong commitment and involvement in a local church. The church provides the daily spiritual direction and equipping necessary for a truly godly marriage.

FamilyLife is committed to changing the destiny of the family and providing quality resources to churches and individuals to build distinctively Christian marriages. In addition to **The HomeBuilders Couples Series®**, we offer:

- "FamilyLife Today," our daily radio show with Dennis Rainey. This half-hour broadcast offers biblical, practical tips for building your family with a foundation in Christ.
- The FamilyLife Marriage Conference, a weekend getaway for couples to learn how to experience oneness in their marriages.
- The FamilyLife Parenting Conference, in which parents learn practical ways to raise their children to know and love the Lord.
- The Urban Family Conference, a shorter version of the FamilyLife Marriage Conference that is geared to the needs of African-American families.
- Numerous materials to help you grow as a family and reach out to others.

HOW TO LEAD A HOMEBUILDERS BIBLE STUDY ELECTIVE

What It Takes to Lead a HomeBuilders Study

You may find that a HomeBuilders study is a bit different from other adult church curriculum you've used. To be specific, *small-group interaction is the foundation for the curriculum.* As class leader you take on the role of "facilitator"—a directive guide who encourages people to think, to discover what Scripture says and to interact with others in the group. The design of these sessions does not call for you to be an authority or a teacher—your job is to help the group members glean biblical truth and apply it to their lives.

In guiding the active participation of your class members, you don't want to let them ramble aimlessly or pool their ignorance. You'll need to familiarize yourself with the material so that you know where the discussion is headed and so you can provide answers when needed. The directions in this leader's guide will help you keep each session moving.

Since this is a series for couples, it will be beneficial for you and your mate to work together to make the course a success. Commit to each other and to God that this study will be a major priority for both of you.

SPECIAL NOTE ABOUT GROUP SIZE: We recommend that a group have no more than 16 people; anything larger begins to inhibit good small-group interaction. If you have a large class, we strongly urge you to divide it into smaller groups for this series and recruit leaders to guide each group. (Each group leader will need his or her own Leader's Guide.)

Using the Leader's Guide

This book and the suggestions we make are designed to cause your creative juices to flow, not cramp your style. You will undoubtedly come up with some distinctive ways to use this material. That's fine. Don't let these recommendations force you into a box.

If, however, you find it difficult to be creative as a leader, this guide will relieve your fears. In it you will find ideas, questions and tips that will help keep the study moving.

Each of the 13 sessions in this study contains the following material, in order:

Leader Notes: This opening section includes detailed instructions and tips for the leader. Answers to questions as well as leader *Tips, Notes* and *Comments* appear in italics to distinguish them from the regular content and questions.

Student Notes: These reproducible pages include all the session questions and are handed out to group members at the beginning of each class. Notes for each session end with a HomeBuilders Project for group members to complete before you meet again.

Format for Each Session

The following outline gives a quick look at how the sessions are structured:

FOCUS: a statement of the overall focus of the session you will be studying.

WARM UP: a time to help people get to know each other, review the past session and begin the new study.

BLUEPRINTS: the biblical content of the session.

HOMEBUILDERS PRINCIPLES: summary points made throughout the study.

MAKE A DATE: a time for couples to decide when they will complete their HomeBuilders Project.

HOMEBUILDERS PROJECT: a 20-30 minute project to be completed at home before the next session.

RECOMMENDED READING: suggestions for use of several books to get maximum value from the study.

Although this format varies slightly from session to session, you should familiarize yourself with it so that you are aware of the purpose of each segment of the study. Explaining the segments to your class will also aid them in understanding the session's content.

Time Schedule

The time for the actual study is 45-60 minutes. If you have a longer time period available, you will be able to move at a more relaxed pace through each part of the session.

As the people in your class get to know each other better through the small-group interaction, you may find it difficult to complete a session in the time allotted. It is not necessary that every question be covered, since many are intended to stimulate thought, not to result in exhaustive discussion and resolution of every issue. Be sensitive to your use of time and be careful not to make comments about time pressure which will make the group feel rushed. For example:

- When you need to move the discussion to the next item, say something like, "We could probably talk about that question the rest of the day, but let's also consider several other important questions that bear on this issue."
- When it's necessary to reduce or eliminate the time for a question or topic, simply say, "You can see that there are several more questions we could have moved on to discuss, but I felt we were making real progress, so I chose to spend some extra time on the earlier points."

As you prepare and review for each session, you will find that some questions or sections are more relevant to your class than other portions of the study. Pace your study in such a way that those questions which must be addressed are not rushed.

You are the leader of your class and know the needs of the individual couples. But keep in mind that the Holy Spirit will have an agenda for specific couples which you may never know about. As Proverbs 16:9 says, "The mind of man plans his way, but the Lord directs his steps." Do your best to prepare and pray over the session and then leave the results to God.

Be aware of the common tendency to get embroiled in a discussion on one point, and not have time to deal with those which follow (which may be even more significant). Even if an issue is not fully resolved, encourage people to place the topic on hold and move on to the next issues. Often resolution of a "sticky" issue does not fully take place until all facets of a topic have been considered.

If you have 60 minutes to work with, plan at least an additional 15 minutes for fellowship, 5 or 10 minutes of which may precede the study and the remainder afterwards. When you invite people to the class, tell them to plan on the total time. This reduces having people drag in late or rush off early and not get acquainted.

Also, when you announce the study, let people know that it will go for thirteen weeks. People like to know how long they are committing themselves.

The shorter time period available for a Sunday School session can pose a problem in adequately dealing with all the essential concepts in a study. A few minutes digression in a 45 to 60 minute session is harder to recoup than in the longer time period available for an evening small group. Here are three options to consider as ways to ensure the best use of the limited time available:

1. *Eliminate for these weeks the normal singing, announcements, and other activities which are often a part of many adult classes.* Inform class members that you intend to use the full session for learning and fellowship features which are vital to the impact of the study. People who are used to slipping in late may need an extra nudge to get them there on time. The informal fellowship dimension which is vital to helping people feel at home in the group can be done before and after the session. The leader will need to be very sensitive to using that time wisely, since people will have other commitments that keep them from lingering.

2. *If you have 60 minutes or less available, look for ways to condense parts of the actual study to about 45 minutes.* One way to accomplish this is to cut a few questions. Look through each lesson and determine what is most important to cover, and mark the questions that you think could be eliminated. Perhaps you can choose just one question from a **Warm Up** to use, for example.

3. *You can also save time by dividing your class into small groups and assigning specific questions (or verses) to different groups for discussion.* Then have representatives from the small groups report briefly to the whole class. If you have less than eight or nine couples, you could do most discussions with the class as a whole. But if your class is larger, we suggest dividing into groups of three couples each. You could either assign each couple to a permanent group throughout the entire study, or you could divide the class into different groups each week.

In working with small groups in your class, decide in advance if you want to appoint a leader in each group or if you prefer guiding the discussion from up front. If you do want to guide the discussion, you could switch back and forth between having the individuals answer questions to the whole class and answering them just within the small groups.

How the Bible Is Used in This Study

As you proceed through this study, you will notice that the Bible is regarded as the final authority on the issues of life and marriage. Although written centuries ago, this Book still speaks clearly and powerfully about the conflicts and struggles men and women face. The Bible is God's Word and contains His blueprints for building a godly home and for dealing with the practical issues of living.

While Scripture has only one primary interpretation, there may be several appropriate applications. Some of the passages used in this series were not originally written with marriage in mind, but they can be applied practically to the husband-wife relationship.

Encourage each group member to have a Bible with him or her for each session. The *New American Standard Bible*, the *New International Version*® and the *New King James Version* are three excellent English versions which make the Bible easy to understand.

Ground Rules for Each Session

These sessions are designed to be enjoyable and informative—and nonthreatening. Three simple ground rules will help ensure that everyone feels comfortable and gets the most out of the study:

1. Share nothing about your marriage which will embarrass your mate.
2. You may "pass" on any question you do not want to answer.
3. Complete the **HomeBuilders Projects** (questions for each couple to discuss and act on) between each session. Be prepared to share one result at the next group meeting.

Setting Up Your Class

You need a room where everyone can sit comfortably and see and hear each other. Avoid letting couples or individuals sit outside the group; they will not feel included. The seating arrangement is very important to discussion and involvement.

- Chairs should be easily movable to enable formation of small groups, and the room should be large enough to allow couples opportunity to talk "privately."
- Leave adequate open space where people can mingle casually before and after the session.
- Set up chairs around tables or in circles of six to eight. For variety in some sessions, you may want to set the chairs in a large semicircle (with more than one row if necessary). Avoid straight rows that leave people seeing only the backs of heads.

Plan to occasionally use a chalkboard, overhead projector or flip chart to emphasize key points, to focus attention on key questions or Scriptures and/or to place instructions for assignments to be done by individuals, couples or small groups. Be cautious about overusing these tools, as they can set a "classroom" tone which may inhibit some people from full participation.

If you want a comfortable, relaxed setting that encourages people to get to know one another, something to sip and swallow is almost essential. Depending on the time of your meeting, you may find it works well to offer both hot and cold beverages and light "munchies" (donuts, muffins, fruit slices, etc.) as people arrive. Have enough ready to also have something available at the close of the study to encourage people to continue talking with each other for a while.

People to Invite

The concepts in this study will benefit any couple, whether they are newlyweds, engaged, married many years or even just looking ahead to the possibilities of marriage. Leading the class will be easier if your group is made up of couples at generally similar stages in their relationships. The more they have in common, the easier it will be for them to identify with one another and open up in sharing.

On the other hand, it also can be helpful for a couple to gain a fresh viewpoint on marriage by interacting with a couple having significantly different experiences. In other words, if a couple is interested in building and maintaining a strong marriage, they belong in this study.

Expect some people, especially some husbands, to attend the first session wishing they were someplace else. Some will be there just because their mate or another couple nagged them to come. Some may be suspicious of a "Bible" class. Others may be fearful of revealing any weaknesses in their marriage. And some may feel either that their marriages are beyond help or that they do not need any help.

You can dispel a great deal of anxiety and resistance at the first session. Simply begin by mentioning that you know there are probably some who came reluctantly. Share a few reasons people may feel that way, and affirm that regardless of why anyone has come, you are pleased each person is there.

Briefly comment on how the concepts in this study have helped you and your marriage and express your confidence that each person will enjoy the study and benefit from it. Also, assure the group that at no time will anyone be forced to share publicly. What each person shares is his or her choice—no one will be embarrassed.

In spite of such efforts, over the course of the study, some people are likely to have to come to at least some sessions without a partner. Assure these people that you are glad they made the effort to come alone. Make sure you include them in class discussions. When having people meet as couples, consider these alternatives for those without partners:

- Have them meet with another person whose spouse is not present. Encourage them to focus on their own efforts to build their marriages, not talking about what their mates do or don't do.
- Invite them to write answers and reflections to share later with their mates.

Also, the study is definitely targeted at Christians, but many non-Christian couples have participated in it. You may find a non-Christian couple or individual who wants to build a strong marriage and is willing to participate. Welcome the non-Christian into your class and seek to get to know the person during the early weeks of the study.

Sometime during the study, schedule a time to meet with this person or couple privately to explain the principles on which this study is built. Share Christ and offer an opportunity to receive Him as Savior and Lord. We recommend "The Four Spiritual Laws" to help you explain how a person can know God. This information is included in Appendix A.

Suggestions for Guiding the Group Discussions

Keep the focus on what Scripture says, not on you or your ideas—or those of the group members, either. When someone disagrees with Scripture, affirm him or her for wrestling with the issue and point out that some biblical statements are hard to understand or to accept. Encourage the person to keep an open mind on the issue at least through the remainder of the study.

Avoid labeling an answer as "wrong"; doing so can kill the atmosphere for discussion. Encourage a person who gives an incorrect or incomplete answer to look again at the question or the Scripture being explored. Offer a comment such as, "That's really close" or, "There's something else we need to see there." Or ask others in the group to respond.

Getting Everyone to Participate

A good way to encourage a nonparticipator to respond is to ask him or her to share an opinion or a personal experience rather than posing a question that can be answered "yes" or "no" or that requires a specific correct answer.

An overly talkative person can intimidate others from participating. Such behavior can be kept in control by the use of devices that call for responses in a specific manner (and which also help group members get to know little things about each other):

- "I'd like this question to be answered first by the husband of the couple with the next anniversary."
- "...the wife of the couple who had the shortest engagement."
- "...any husband who knows his mother-in-law's maiden name."
- "...anyone who complained about doing last week's project."

Other devices for guiding responses from the class include:

- Go around the class in sequence with each person offering a one-sentence comment about a particular question without repeating what anyone else has said. If the class has more than twelve or fifteen people, select one section of the class to participate in this sharing.
- Ask couples to talk with each other about a question, then ask for a show of hands of the partners who have said the least so far in this session. Then invite volunteers from those who raised their hands to report on their answers.
- Limit answers to one or two sentences—or to 30 seconds each.

Establishing an Environment of Accountability

From the outset, emphasize the importance of completing the HomeBuilders Project after each session. These projects give couples the opportunity to discuss what they've learned and apply it to their lives. The couples who complete these projects will get two or three times as much out of this study as will those who do not.

The most important thing you can do is state at the end of the first session that *at your next meeting you will ask each couple to share something they learned from the* **HomeBuilders Project.** *Then at the next session, follow through on your promise.* If they know you are going to hold them accountable, they'll be more motivated to complete the projects. And they'll be glad they did!

Remember to make this an environment of *friendly* accountability. You should emphasize how beneficial the projects are, and how much persons will grow in their marriage relationships if they complete them. State that you are not here to pressure or to condemn, but to help. And when you begin the following session by asking couples to tell what they learned from the project, do it with an attitude of encouragement and forgiveness. Don't seek to embarrass anyone.

One way to establish friendly accountability and to help couples know each other better is to pair up the couples in your class and assign them to be prayer partners or accountability partners. Have them call each other at some point in between class sessions to exchange prayer requests and to see if they've completed their projects.

Another possibility to consider is making a special effort to hold the men accountable to be the initiator in completing the projects. You'd need to commit yourself to calling the men between sessions.

Another option is to divide the class into two or more teams. Each week require couples to turn in an affidavit that they completed their project. Tabulate the results. The team with the lowest completion rate must provide some agreed upon benefit (preferably edible) for the winning team at the end of the series.

HomeBuilders Principle #1:

It is only as you yield and submit your life to God, obey His Word and deny yourself that you can experience intimacy and build a godly marriage.

HomeBuilders Principle #2:

Oneness in marriage involves complete unity with each other.

HomeBuilders Principle #3:

In order to achieve oneness, a couple must share a strong commitment to God's purpose for marriage.

HomeBuilders Principle #4:

When we yield to God and build together from His blueprints, we begin the process of experiencing oneness.

HomeBuilders Principle #5:

The basis for my acceptance of my mate is faith in God's character and trustworthiness.

HomeBuilders Principle #6:

A godly marriage is not created by finding a perfect, flawless person, but is created by allowing God's perfect love and acceptance to flow through one imperfect person—you—toward another imperfect person—your mate.

HomeBuilders Principle #7:
A godly marriage is established and experienced as we leave, cleave and become one flesh.

HomeBuilders Principle #8:
Only spiritual Christians can have a hope of building godly homes.

HomeBuilders Principle #9:
The home built by God requires both the husband and wife to yield to the Holy Spirit in every area of their lives.

HomeBuilders Principle #10:
The heritage you were handed is not as important as the legacy you will leave.

HomeBuilders Principle #11:
The legacy you leave is determined by the life you live.

HomeBuilders Principle #12:
Your marriage should leave a legacy of love that will influence future generations.

Men Only

HomeBuilders Principle for Men #1:
A husband who is becoming a servant-leader is one who is in the process of denying himself daily for his wife.

HomeBuilders Principle for Men #2:

The husband who is becoming an unselfish lover of his wife is one who is putting his wife's needs above his own.

HomeBuilders Principle for Men #3:

The husband who is becoming a caring head of his house is one who encourages his wife to grow and become all that God intended her to be.

Women Only

HomeBuilders Principle for Women #1:

Becoming a successful wife requires that a woman make her husband her number two priority after her relationship with God.

HomeBuilders Principle for Women #2:

The wife who is becoming an unselfish lover of her husband is one who is putting her husband's needs above her own.

HomeBuilders Principle for Women #3:

In order for a husband to successfully lead, he must have a wife who willingly submits to his leadership.

HomeBuilders Principle for Women #4:

A successful wife is one who respects her husband.

INTRODUCTION

About The HomeBuilders Couples Series®

What Is the Purpose of the HomeBuilders Series?

Do you remember the first time you fell in love? That junior high—or elementary school—"crush" stirred your affections with little or no effort on your part. We use the term "falling in love" to describe the phenomenon of suddenly discovering our emotions have been captured by someone delightful.

Unfortunately, our society tends to make us think that all loving relationships should be equally effortless. Thus, millions of couples, Christians included, approach their marriages certain that the emotions they feel will carry them through any difficulties. And millions of couples quickly learn that a good marriage does not automatically happen.

Otherwise intelligent people, who would not think of buying a car, investing money, or even going to the grocery store without some initial planning, enter into marriage with no plan of how to make their marriage succeed.

But God has already provided the plan, a set of blueprints for a truly godly marriage. His plan is designed to enable two people to grow together in a mutually satisfying relationship, and then to look beyond their own marriage to others. Ignoring this plan leads to isolation and separation between husband and wife—the pattern so evident in the majority of homes today. Even when great energy is expended, failure to follow God's blueprints results in wasted effort, bitter disappointment—and, in far too many cases, divorce.

In response to this need in marriages today, FamilyLife of Campus Crusade for Christ created a popular series of small-group Bible studies for couples called **The HomeBuilders Couples Series®**. The series has now been adapted for larger groups such as adult Sunday School classes. Now you can lead a class of adults in a study designed to answer one question for couples:

How do you build a distinctively Christian marriage?

It is our hope that in answering this question with the biblical blueprints for building a home, we will see the development of growing, thriving marriages filled with the love of Jesus Christ.

FamilyLife is committed to strengthening your family. We hope **The HomeBuilders Couples Series®** will assist you and your church as it equips couples in building godly homes.

How the Is Bible Used in This Study

As you proceed through this study, you will notice that the Bible is regarded as the final authority on the issues of life and marriage. Although written centuries ago, this Book still speaks clearly and powerfully about the conflicts and struggles men and women face. The Bible is God's Word and contains His blueprints for building a godly home and for dealing with the practical issues of living.

While Scripture has only one primary interpretation, there may be several appropriate applications. Some of the passages used in this series were not originally written with marriage in mind, but they can be applied practically to the husband-wife relationship.

Each group member is encouraged to have a Bible with him or her for each session. *The New American Standard Bible*, the *New International Version*® and the *New King James Version* are three excellent English versions which make the Bible easy to understand.

Ground Rules for Each Session

These sessions are designed to be enjoyable and informative—and nonthreatening. Three simple ground rules will help ensure that everyone feels comfortable and gets the most out of the study:

1. Share nothing about your marriage which will embarrass your mate.
2. You may "pass" on any question you do not want to answer.
3. Complete the **HomeBuilders Projects** (questions for each couple to discuss and act on) between each session. Be prepared to share one result at the next group meeting.

HomeBuilders Principle #1:

It is only as you yield and submit your life to God, obey His Word and deny yourself that you can experience intimacy and build a godly marriage.

HomeBuilders Principle #2:

Oneness in marriage involves complete unity with each other.

HomeBuilders Principle #3:

In order to achieve oneness, a couple must share a strong commitment to God's purpose for marriage.

HomeBuilders Principle #4:

When we yield to God and build together from His blueprints, we begin the process of experiencing oneness.

HomeBuilders Principle #5:

The basis for my acceptance of my mate is faith in God's character and trustworthiness.

HomeBuilders Principle #6:

A godly marriage is not created by finding a perfect, flawless person, but is created by allowing God's perfect love and acceptance to flow through one imperfect person—you—toward another imperfect person—your mate.

HomeBuilders Principle #7:

A godly marriage is established and experienced as we leave, cleave and become one flesh.

HomeBuilders Principle #8:

Only spiritual Christians can have a hope of building godly homes.

HomeBuilders Principle #9:

The home built by God requires both the husband and wife to yield to the Holy Spirit in every area of their lives.

HomeBuilders Principle #10:

The heritage you were handed is not as important as the legacy you will leave.

HomeBuilders Principle #11:

The legacy you leave is determined by the life you live.

HomeBuilders Principle #12:

Your marriage should leave a legacy of love that will influence future generations.

Men Only

HomeBuilders Principle for Men #1:

A husband who is becoming a servant-leader is one who is in the process of denying himself daily for his wife.

HomeBuilders Principle for Men #2:
The husband who is becoming an unselfish lover of his wife is one who is putting his wife's needs above his own.

HomeBuilders Principle for Men #3:
The husband who is becoming a caring head of his house is one who encourages his wife to grow and become all that God intended her to be.

Women Only

HomeBuilders Principle for Women #1:
Becoming a successful wife requires that a woman make her husband her number two priority after her relationship with God.

HomeBuilders Principle for Women #2:
The wife who is becoming an unselfish lover of her husband is one who is putting her husband's needs above her own.

HomeBuilders Principle for Women #3:
In order for a husband to successfully lead, he must have a wife who willingly submits to his leadership.

HomeBuilders Principle for Women #4:
A successful wife is one who respects her husband.

SESSION 1

Overcoming Isolation: Identifying the Problem

OBJECTIVES

You will help your group members adopt God's blueprints for marriage as you guide them to:

* Create some anticipation for your study together;
* Share enjoyable experiences from their marriages; and
* Identify selfishness as the cause of isolation in marriage.

COMMENTS

1. This session sets the tone for the study. Take time to become familiar with every item in the session as well as the tips on leading the group found in the introduction to this leader's guide.
2. Be sure you duplicate copies of the reproducible handouts, one for each individual. You will also want to have a Bible and extra pens and pencils for class members who may have forgotten to bring them.

    Option: Several days before the first session, personally distribute the introductory page, "About **The HomeBuilders Couples Series®**." Ask class members to read the introductory article to lay the groundwork for the study.

STARTING THE FIRST SESSION

1. Start the session on time, even if everyone is not there yet.
2. Briefly share a few positive feelings about leading this study:

    * Express your interest in strengthening your own marriage.
    * Admit that your marriage is not perfect.

- State that the concepts in this study have been helpful in your marriage.
- Recognize that various individuals or couples may have been reluctant to come (pressured by spouse or friend, wary of a "Christian" group, sensitive about problems with marriage, stress in schedule that makes it difficult to set aside the time for this study, etc.)
- Thank group members for their interest and willingness to participate.

3. Hand out copies of the introductory article, "About **The HomeBuilders Couples Series®**" if you haven't already done so, and give a quick overview of the study. Briefly point out three or four topics and the benefits of studying them. Don't be afraid of doing a little selling here—people need to know how they personally are going to profit from the study. They also need to know where this study will take them, especially if they are even a little bit apprehensive about the group.

4. Explain the format for each session in no more than two or three minutes, using Session 1 as your example. Each session contains the following components:

    Focus—A capsule statement of the main point of the session.

    Warm Up—A time to get better acquainted with each other and to begin thinking of the session topic.

    Blueprints—Discovering God's purposes and plans for marriage.

    HomeBuilders Principles—Summary points made throughout the study.

    Make a Date—A time to decide when during the week they will complete the **HomeBuilders Project**.

    HomeBuilders Project—Half an hour during the week when husband and wife interact with the implications of what was learned. These times are really the heart of the study.

    Recommended Reading—Books that couples can read together to get maximum benefit from the study.

5. Call attention to the "ground rules" for the sessions:
    a. Share nothing about your marriage which will embarrass your mate.
    b. You may "pass" on any question you do not want to answer.
    c. Complete the **HomeBuilders Project** (questions for each couple to discuss and act on) between each session. Share one result at the next group meeting.

Note: In the sections to come, material that appears on the reproducible handouts is presented in regular type and added material for the leader appears in italics.

Focus

Selfishness and isolation are the major obstacles
to building oneness and a godly marriage.

Warm-Up

*Student is on
page 39.*

(20-25 Minutes)

The tone for the study is set in these opening minutes, so take time to help everyone relax and open up with each other. More serious items which come later will not be seen as threatening once people know each other and develop a measure of transparency within the group.

Start the sharing by explaining that one of the purposes of the study is to help everyone enjoy being together and to learn from one another's experiences. Begin by telling about three incidents from your own marriage, taking no more than one minute per incident:

1. *Where and when you met;*
2. *One fun or unique date before your marriage;*
3. *One humorous or romantic time from your honeymoon or early married life.*

It might be a good idea to have the spouse who is not leading the session tell these stories.

Set a tone of openness by sharing at a personal level, giving enough detail and color to make the stories come alive. Avoid being too reserved. Remember, your example will set the tone for honesty, humor and length.

To help people relax and enjoy talking with others in the class, each couple will be allowed up to three minutes (assign a timekeeper) to share the same three incidents. Distribute copies of the Session 1 handouts.

Instruct each couple to take three minutes to meet together to decide what incidents they want to share and who will do the talking. Suggest that in most marriages one person is a "storyteller" and the other is a "news reporter." The news reporter just gives the bare facts. The storyteller gives the detail and color. Ask that the "storyteller" partner be the one to share. Warn them again not to share anything that would embarrass their mates.

Explain that as each couple shares, everyone is to write the names of the couple and one word or phrase which refers to an interesting incident about them. Ask for a couple to volunteer to go first, introducing themselves and then telling their stories.

Keep the speakers to the time limit so the sharing does not drag.

For this sharing, divide the class into groups of up to five couples per group. If you have less than 45 minutes for your study, reduce the time for each couple to share. If some people are present without their spouses, pair them with other "singles" and/or with you and your spouse.

As each couple or individual shares, write the names of the couple and one word or phrase which refers to an interesting incident about them.

_____
_____
_____
_____
_____
_____
_____

Conclude the sharing by once again explaining the purpose of the Blueprints section.

(25-35 Minutes)

The purpose of the questions in the first part of the Blueprints is to go below the symptoms to discover that selfishness is the root cause that divides people.

One caution is appropriate here before you move your group into this discussion: this Blueprints section talks about selfishness and can become a negative discussion. Be sure to keep your group moving through this section and get them to the solution found later in the session. The purpose of starting with the problem is to get to the root cause of mediocre marriages today and to create a need for the solution introduced at the conclusion of this study and explored thoroughly in the next session.

A. A Cause of Failure in Marriage
(10-15 Minutes)

No one starts out intending to fail in a marriage, but many do. It seems that few succeed at building a marriage that stands the test of time.

1. Why do you think couples are so naturally close during dating—and then often so distant after they marry?

    _____
    _____

Answer: Things that initially attract you to your mate may end up irritating you after you become more familiar with each other. Differences between you and your mate become magnified. Couples often work harder to please each other and to open up to each other during courtship than they do after they are married.

Tip: Encourage people to write down the ideas shared, since they may want to come back to certain points as they work through the HomeBuilders Project during the week. Ask everyone to think for a moment of the enjoyable experiences they told about earlier and then to consider that marriages which end in divorce are not the only failed marriages; many other couples continue to live together, enduring an emotional divorce.

2. One of the main reasons people get married is to find intimacy—a close, personal relationship with another person. Yet it does not seem to come naturally. Why do you think this is true?

    _____

    _____

    _____

Answer: One common problem is selfishness—both partners going in their own directions and wanting things their own way.

3. What insight for failure in marriage might be implied from Isaiah 53:6a?

    _____

    _____

    _____

Answer: "going your own way," which is selfishness.

Comment: "Many passages dealing with the broader issues of problems in human living can provide us with clues about the cause of marital problems."

4. It is easier to see selfishness in your mate than in yourself. What are at least three ways you struggle with selfishness in your marriage?

    _____

    _____

    _____

Tip: Share your own responses to Question 4. Then instruct everyone to take two or three minutes alone to list ways in which he or she struggles with selfishness. Alert them that you will ask everyone to share one item from their list.

Student is on page 40.

B. Results of Going Your Own Way
(10 Minutes)

1. How have the above examples of "going your own way" affected your marriage? Be specific.

   _____

   _____

   _____

   Tip: *If some people share very vague answers, i.e., "It caused problems," encourage them to think of specific evidence they noticed: attitudes, actions, communication, etc.*

   Also, if some people assert that it is not wrong to look out for themselves—that they have the right to do some things that they want ("I work hard all week and deserve a chance to..."), avoid trying to label that activity as good or bad. Just rephrase Question 1: "How has that activity affected your marriage? Has it helped build intimacy with your mate, or has it created distance?"

2. Selfishness in a relationship leads to isolation. (Instead of the closeness we want, we end up being separated from each other.)

   `i-so-`la-tion (n) The condition of being alone, separated, solitary, set apart (from the Latin *insulatus,* made into an island). (*The American Heritage Dictionary*)

   Why is isolation to be feared in marriage?

   _____

   _____

   _____

   Answer: *Isolation is the opposite of intimacy and oneness. Isolation involves building walls of separation rather than bridges of communication. Isolation results in misunderstanding, pride, frustration, sexual and emotional dissatisfaction and all the other symptoms of a troubled marriage.*

   Comment: *"Isolation is found not just in troubled marriages. It exists to a greater or lesser degree in every relationship where people 'go their own way.'"*

3. Even stronger than fear of isolation is the fear of being rejected. Why do you think this is so? Why are people willing to tolerate isolation, rather than working to build oneness and harmony in marriage?

   _____

   _____

   _____

   _____

Tip: Ask for someone who has not had a chance to answer one of the previous questions to share thoughts on Question 3.

The above issues lead us to consider these questions:

- How can a couple defeat selfishness and thus avoid being isolated from one another?
- How can a couple build a home that will withstand the pressures that are destroying marriages today?

The answer is found in a story Jesus told about two attempts to build a home.

C. The Solution to Isolation in Marriage
(5-10 Minutes)

Student is on page 41.

Note: This segment is designed to help participants recognize that the solution to isolation in their marriages is to be committed to hearing and obeying the biblical blueprints for marriage. The storms in this story can be compared to the problems that arise in a marriage as a result of selfishness and isolation. This parable does not deal specifically with selfishness, but it does lay the essential foundation for approaching the biblical teachings on the subject. Encourage participants to complete the chart on their Blueprints page as you read aloud from Matthew 7:24-27 the story Jesus told.

Read Jesus' story in Matthew 7:24-27 and complete this chart:

What were the two foundations?		
Answer:	*Rock*	*Sand*
How were the two men described?		
Answer:	*Wise*	*Foolish*
Both men heard Christ's words; what was each man's response?		
Answer:	*The wise man is compared to those who act on what Christ says*	*The foolish man is compared to those who do not.*
What was the ultimate result?		
Answer:	*The wise man's house stood through the storm*	*The foolish man's house was destroyed*

Tip: After you complete the reading, ask volunteers to call out the answer to each question on the chart. Then have each person privately mark which statement is closest to his or her response to the story. Assure them that they will not have to share the answers with anyone in the group, but they will be asked to compare answers with their mates as part of the HomeBuilders Project during the week.

Which of these statements comes closest to matching your response to this story?

- ❑ It's a nice story, but I don't see how it fits my marriage.
- ❑ I get the point about putting good advice into practice, but I'm not convinced Christ's advice is best.
- ❑ I think a lot of what Jesus said is helpful and I'll consider it.
- ❑ I'm willing to follow Christ's teachings in my marriage.
- ❑ I enthusiastically embrace Christ's teachings in my marriage.

Summarize the point this story makes for your life and marriage.

_____

_____

_____

_____

_____

Student is on page 42.

Make a date with your mate to meet in the next few days to complete *HomeBuilders Project #1.* This will aid you as a couple in continuing the process of building your marriage. Your leader will ask you at the next session to share one thing from this experience.

_____   _____   _____

Date   Time   Location

*Have couples look at the **Make a Date** section. Instruct them to take a few moments and set a time this week when they will complete HomeBuilders Project #1 together. (See Student Handouts.) Encourage them to set aside 20 to 30 minutes in which to respond to the items individually and discuss their answers together.*

Each HomeBuilders Project is vitally important for couples to do together during the week. Emphasize that this is not homework to earn a passing grade, but a highly significant time of interaction that will improve communication, understanding and enjoyment as you build your marriage according to God's blueprints.

Point out that some questions focus on potentially sensitive issues. The intention is not to start arguments, but to stimulate honest reflection and interaction. While not every question will affect every couple in the same way, the time spent thinking and talking will be more than worthwhile for any couple.

Remind the group that at the next session you will ask each couple to share one thing they discovered or discussed during the HomeBuilders Project. Also, remind group members to bring their calendars to each session as an aid in scheduling their next date with their mates.

Option: *You may want to pair each couple with another couple with whom they will agree to be accountable to complete the HomeBuilders Projects. Have the couples tell each other when they will be doing the projects. The couples can then call each other later to see how the projects went, or you can have them meet with each other for a few minutes at the start of the next session.*

Call attention to the Recommended Reading section. The books listed at the end of each session are not required, but are recommended to reinforce and expand the concepts dealt with in the group session. Encourage couples to locate this book and read the featured chapter(s) before the next session. One effective idea is for one spouse to read aloud to the other, either in the morning before going to work or in the evening before going to sleep.

Staying Close by Dennis Rainey.

This book by the director of FamilyLife expands on the subjects covered in this study and in our FamilyLife Marriage Conference. Chapters 1-2 will help you consider further the issues discussed in this session.

Lead the group in a closing prayer. If you know the group members well enough, you may feel comfortable having them spend a few minutes praying for one another's concerns about selfishness and isolation in the coming week.

Provide light refreshments and invite people to linger and chat with each other. Informal opportunities to build relationships are a key ingredient in the success of this study. If necessary, shorten the study time in this session so that people do not feel pressed to leave quickly.

SESSION 1

Overcoming Isolation: Identifying the Problem

Selfishness and isolation are the major obstacles to building oneness and a godly marriage.

One purpose of this study is to help everyone enjoy learning from one another's experiences. Begin by telling about three incidents from your own marriage, taking no more than one minute per incident:

1.   Where and when you met;
2.   One fun or unique date before your marriage;
3.   One humorous or romantic time from your honeymoon or early married life.

As each couple shares, write the names of the couple and one word or phrase which refers to an interesting incident about them.

_____

_____

_____

A. A Cause of Failure in Marriage

No one starts out intending to fail in a marriage, but many do. It seems that few succeed at building a marriage that stands the test of time.

1. Why do you think couples are so naturally close during dating—and then often so distant after they marry?

    _____

    _____

2. One of the main reasons people get married is to find intimacy—a close, personal relationship with another person. Yet it does not seem to come naturally. Why do you think this is true?

    _____

    _____

    _____

3. What insight for failure in marriage might be implied from Isaiah 53:6a?

    _____

    _____

    _____

4. It is easier to see selfishness in your mate than in yourself. What are at least three ways you struggle with selfishness in your marriage?

    _____

    _____

    _____

B. Results of Going Your Own Way

1. How have the above examples of "going your own way" affected your marriage? Be specific.

    _____

    _____

    _____

2. Selfishness in a relationship leads to isolation. (Instead of the closeness we want, we end up being separated from each other.)

    `i-so-`la-tion (n) The condition of being alone, separated, solitary, set apart (from the Latin *insulatus,* made into an island). (*The American Heritage Dictionary*)

Why is isolation to be feared in marriage?

_____

_____

_____

3. Even stronger than fear of isolation is fear of being rejected. Why do you think this is so? Why are people willing to tolerate isolation, rather than working to build oneness and harmony in marriage?

    _____

    _____

    _____

The above issues lead us to consider these questions:

*   How can a couple defeat selfishness and thus avoid being isolated from one another?
*   How can a couple build a home that will withstand the pressures that are destroying marriages today?

The answer is found in a story Jesus told about building a home.

C. The Solution to Isolation in Marriage

Read Jesus' story in Matthew 7:24-27 and complete the chart:

What were the two foundations?	
How were the two men described?	
Both men heard Christ's words; what was each man's response?	
What was the ultimate result?	

Which of these statements comes closest to matching your response to this story?
*   ❑ It's a nice story, but I don't see how it fits my marriage.
*   ❑ I get the point about putting good advice into practice, but I'm not convinced Christ's advice is best.
*   ❑ I think a lot of what Jesus said is helpful and I'll consider it.
*   ❑ I'm willing to follow Christ's teachings in my marriage.
*   ❑ I enthusiastically embrace Christ's teachings in my marriage.

Summarize the point this story makes for your life and marriage:

_____

_____

_____

_____

_____

Make a date with your mate to meet in the next few days to complete **HomeBuilders Project #1**. This will aid you as a couple in continuing the process of building your marriage. Your leader will ask you at the next session to share one thing from this experience.

_____   _____   _____

Date   Time   Location

Staying Close by Dennis Rainey.

This book by the director of FamilyLife expands on the subjects covered in this study and in the FamilyLife Marriage Conference. Chapters 1-2 will help you consider further the issues discussed in this session.

Individually: 5-10 Minutes

Write your answers to these questions.

1. Recall a moment during the past year when you felt close to your mate.

    _____
    _____
    _____

    _____

2. During that time, how was selfishness defeated?

    _____
    _____
    _____

3. Most of us find it difficult to admit when we are being selfish. It is usually easier to recognize our selfishness by looking back at times when we pressed to get our own way. When was a time that you allowed selfishness to control your interaction with your mate?

    _____
    _____
    _____

    _____

Interact As a Couple: 15-20 Minutes

1. Complete any activity from the first session that you may not have had time to complete or want to study further. Share what was most meaningful to you in Session 1.
2. Compare your responses to the questions about Jesus' story of the two builders. Whether you answered identically or differently, share your reasons.
3. Share your answers to the above questions and the discoveries that you made in answering them.
4. Close your time together by praying for one another.

Remember to bring your calendar for **Make a Date** to the next class session.

SESSION 2

Overcoming Isolation: Defeating the Problem

OBJECTIVES

You will help your group members adopt God's blueprints for marriage as you guide them to:

- Affirm their awareness that God has a plan for overcoming isolation and selfishness in marriage; and
- Choose a specific step to take to work on defeating selfishness.

COMMENTS

1. Session 1 focused on problems in a marriage. This session begins exploring God's blueprints for defeating selfishness and isolation. Be sensitive to those individuals or couples who struggle with accepting God's purposes as their own. Your warmth and acceptance can have a significant role in someone becoming willing to really consider the principles of these sessions.

2. You may wish to have extra Bibles for any who did not bring theirs.

3. Again, light refreshments as people arrive help set a tone of friendly anticipation. And many would find name tags helpful.

4. If someone joins the class for the first time at this session, give a summary of the main thrust of Session 1 as people are gathering. Also, be sure to introduce those who do not know each other and assist them in beginning some informal conversation. If time permits, you may wish to start a little early and have each new couple share an incident from the **Warm Up** in Session 1.

Defeating selfishness and isolation is essential in
building oneness and a godly marriage.

(15-25 Minutes)

*To help people relax and regain feelings of openness, the following game can help. It is planned
to allow people to work together at a task, helping them feel positive about others in the group.*

*Divide the group into at least two teams: men versus women! If you have more than seven
or eight on a team, divide into smaller groups. Explain the game thoroughly before starting.*

You will need the following for the game:

- *Two or more pads of 8½ x 11-inch paper and two or more pencils (one pad and
  pencil for each team);*
- *Two or more areas that have a flat surface (table or chair) that a group of four to
  seven men or women can gather around;*
- *A list of the words on a sheet of paper. See below.*
- *A place to stand that is equal in distance from all groups and is clear for people to
  run back and forth from their group (this game can and should get lively).*

*The game is "Paper Charades." Each team will send one representative to you to start
the game. You will show representatives the first item on your list of words. They will then
return to their teams and draw a picture to lead their teams to guess the word. The person
drawing the picture (representative) cannot speak any words or make any sounds. As soon as
a team guesses correctly, another team member will come to you, tell you the correct word and
get the next word. The first team to guess all the words on the list is the winner and should be
rewarded appropriately (perhaps by having the losers prepare and serve refreshments at the
next session).*

Be sure to cover your list until the person has given you the correct word. Then point to the next word in the list, keeping the remaining words covered. Use the following words as time allows, making sure you start with the simple objects (the first six) and conclude with "concepts" (the last four). Explain that the simple words will be completed rather fast, so speed is the key to victory. The concepts are much harder and thus will take longer. Be aware of your time limit. If time is short, skip several of the words.

> *hammer*
> *roof*
> *ladder*
> *toilet*
> *foundation*
> *blueprints*
> *honeymoon*
> *romance*
> *memories*
> *intimacy*

When you finish the game, ask the groups what all the words had in common. Most likely, they have already noticed that all the words had something to do with building a house. "Building" on that theme, conclude this Warm Up by instructing everyone to share with their team one insight they gained from completing the HomeBuilders' Project during the past week. Then have people rejoin their mates for the remainder of the session.

(30-35 Minutes)

A. The Hope for Defeating Selfishness and Isolation
(10-15 minutes)

Student is on page 53.

Tip: *Distribute copies of the Session 2 handouts. Read aloud HomeBuilders Principle #1.*

HOMEBUILDERS PRINCIPLE #1:

It is only as you yield and submit your life to God, obey His Word and deny yourself that you can experience intimacy and build a godly marriage.

Tip: Divide the class into three sections and assign the people in each section one of the three Scripture passages listed on the page. Instruct them to work in pairs or trios to find the answer that their assigned passage gives to Question 1. Allow two or three minutes for people to read and talk about the answer. Then invite volunteers from each section to share what they discovered.

1. If success in life—and marriage—rests on doing what Christ said, read the following Scriptures and discover what He said about defeating selfishness.
    John 12:24,25

    _____

    Answer: It is necessary to die to our own desires in order to find the key to real living.

    Luke 14:27-30

    _____

    Answer: It is necessary to consider the cost in a relationship and to be willing to pay what it takes to make the relationship work well.

    Mark 10:43-45

    _____

    Answer: It is necessary to serve in order to build anything great.

2. How do these three statements by Christ apply to defeating selfishness and isolation in marriage?

    _____

    In your marriage?

    _____

    Tip: Share some practical ways you've used those principles in your marriage. Then invite volunteers to share their own thoughts.

3. To pay the price, to die to self and to serve your mate—these are hard things to do. Read John 6:60,61,66-69 to find two different responses to Jesus' teachings. Summarize the two responses in the boxes below:

1.	2.

Answer: 1. Many questioned, grumbled and decided not to follow Jesus. 2. But Peter affirmed his belief that Jesus spoke words of life.

Which response is closest to your reaction to Jesus' instructions about defeating selfishness?

_____

Tip: It is likely that some people in the class are struggling with some of the truths in this session. Assure them you have also had times of questioning, but encourage them to follow Peter's example. Stress the value of keeping themselves open to discovering that following Jesus' teaching is truly a great way to find real life and fulfillment in marriage.

4. Read 1 Peter 3:8-12. List things you should do when you feel your mate is being selfish.

_____

Tip: Invite people to call out the actions this passage instructs us to do. List these on the chalkboard, a large sheet of paper, or an overhead transparency. After compiling the list, ask, "How many of us are supposed to follow these instructions?" People should find the answer in verse 8: "all of you."

Tip: Share your own response. Then ask people to write their answers down, indicating at least one specific action they feel they need to take to obey these instructions.

5. What point from these verses do you need to obey in your marriage? What do you need to do?

_____

Tip: Share your own response. Then ask people to write their answers down, indicating at least one specific action they feel they need to take to obey these instructions. After two or three minutes, ask volunteers to share what they have written.

Student is on page 54.

B. Applying Truth to Marriage
(20 Minutes)

This segment engages participants in looking together at the Scriptures just discussed, then sharing ideas about specific actions they can take to apply these truths in their marriages. Encourage people that, while they should try to think of specific situations in which they need to consider and implement these actions, they should not divulge private matters which could embarrass their mates.

If you have more than ten people in your class, divide into two or more groups of at least five people each. Groups look at the Scriptures listed and share their completions to statements 1 and 2. Question 3 should be answered privately. If group members have become comfortable in sharing with each other, invite volunteers to share their responses to Question 3. Hearing someone else's answer can help some people move toward taking action themselves. Then have group members complete Question 4 together.

1. Review John 12:24,25; Luke 14:27-30; or Mark 10:43-45. Finish this sentence: When I'm being selfish, I need to...

   _____

2. Review 1 Peter 3:8-12. Finish this sentence: When my mate is being selfish, I need to...

   _____

3. What one thing will I do this week to show an unselfish attitude toward my mate and obey the words of Christ?

   _____

4. Living in victory over selfishness is a lifelong process. A husband or wife needs the guidance of God's Word. In the passage below, underline the three building blocks which produce solid benefits in a home.

   > "By <u>wisdom</u> a house is built,
   > and by <u>understanding</u> it is established;
   > and by <u>knowledge</u> the rooms are filled
   > with all precious and pleasant riches"
   > (Proverbs 24:3,4).

Scripture provides the raw materials, the building blocks that we need to build a marriage marked by oneness and harmony instead of isolation. The remaining sessions of this first study will explore the blueprints found in God's Word for building your home. Your discovery and application of these truths will result in a home that is built and filled ("established") with *all* precious and pleasant riches!

Tip: Call the group back together and emphasize the last phrase of Proverbs 24:4. Be certain that this session ends on a positive note. People do need to know that there is hope for wonderful benefits to those who follow God's blueprints.

Make a Date

Student is on page 55.

Make a date with your mate to meet in the next few days to complete *HomeBuilders Project #2*. This will aid you as a couple in continuing the process of building your marriage. Your leader will ask you at the next session to share one thing from this experience.

_____   _____   _____
Date   Time   Location

Ask each couple to look at the Make a Date section of the study guide, and to agree on a time this week to complete HomeBuilders Project #2 together. Encourage them to set aside 20 to 30 minutes to respond to the items individually and discuss their answers together. Remind them to save their Blueprint handouts in order to review and compare their responses at that time.

Each HomeBuilders Project is absolutely essential for couples to do together during the week. This is not homework to pass a test, but a highly significant time of interaction that will improve communication and understanding as you build your marriage according to God's blueprints. The time spent thinking and talking will be more than worthwhile for any couple.

Remind the class that at the next session you will ask each couple to share one thing they discovered or discussed during the HomeBuilders Project. Also, remind group members to bring their calendars to the next session as an aid in scheduling their next date with their mates.

Option: If you have paired couples together to be accountable to complete the HomeBuilders Projects, have the couples tell each other when they will be doing the project this week. The couples can then call each other later to see how the projects went, or you can have them meet with each other for a few minutes at the start of the next session.

Remind everyone to help their mates this week in carrying out their planned action to overcome selfishness and isolation.

Call attention to the Recommended Reading section. The books listed at the end of each session are recommended to reinforce and expand the concepts dealt with in the group session. Encourage couples to locate this book and read the featured chapter before the next session.

Staying Close by Dennis Rainey.

This book by the director of FamilyLife expands on the subjects covered in this study and in our FamilyLife Marriage Conference. Chapter 3 will help you consider further the issues discussed in this session.

Lead the group in a closing prayer. If group members show signs of feeling comfortable with each other, have them form small groups and pray for one another's intentions to overcome selfishness and isolation in the coming week. Assure people that no one should feel pressured to pray aloud, so moments of silent prayer are certainly appropriate.

Provide light refreshments and invite people to linger and chat with each other.

SESSION 2

Overcoming Isolation: Defeating the Problem

Defeating selfishness and isolation is essential in building oneness and a godly marriage.

A. The Hope for Defeating Selfishness and Isolation

HOMEBUILDERS PRINCIPLE #1:

It is only as you yield and submit your life to God, obey His Word and deny yourself that you can experience intimacy and build a godly marriage.

1. If success in life—and marriage—rests on doing what Christ said, read the following Scriptures and discover what He said about defeating selfishness.
   John 12:24,25

   _____

   Luke 14:27-30

   _____

   Mark 10:43-45

   _____

2. How do these three statements by Christ apply to defeating selfishness and isolation in marriage? In **your** marriage?

   _____

3. To pay the price, to die to self and to serve your mate—these are hard things to do. Read John 6:60,61,66-69 to find two different responses to Jesus' teachings. Summarize the two responses in the boxes below:

1.	2.

   Which response is closest to your reaction to Jesus' instructions about defeating selfishness?

   _____

4. Read 1 Peter 3:8-12. List things you should do when you feel your mate is being selfish.

   _____

5. What point from these verses do you need to obey in your marriage? What do you need to do?

   _____

B. Applying Truth to Marriage

1. Review John 12:24,25; Luke 14:27-30; or Mark 10:43-45. Finish this sentence: When I'm being selfish, I need to...

   _____

2. Review 1 Peter 3:8-12. Finish this sentence: When my mate is being selfish, I need to...

   _____

3. What one thing will I do this week to show an unselfish attitude toward my mate and obey the words of Christ?

   _____

4. Living in victory over selfishness is a lifelong process. A husband or wife needs the guidance of God's Word. In the passage below, underline the three building blocks which produce solid benefits in a home.

"By wisdom a house is built,
and by understanding it is established;
and by knowledge the rooms are filled
with all precious and pleasant riches"
(Proverbs 24:3,4).

Scripture provides the raw materials, the building blocks that we need to build a marriage marked by oneness and harmony instead of isolation. The remaining sessions of this study will explore the blueprints found in God's Word for building your home. Your discovery and application of these truths will result in a home that is built and filled ("established") with **all** precious and pleasant riches!

Make a date with your mate to meet in the next few days to complete **HomeBuilders Project #2**. This will aid you as a couple in continuing the process of building your marriage. Your leader will ask you at the next session to share one thing from this experience.

Date	Time	Location

Staying Close by Dennis Rainey.

This book by the director of FamilyLife expands on the subjects covered in this study and in our FamilyLife Marriage Conference. Chapter 3 will help you consider further the issues discussed in this session.

Individually: 5-10 Minutes

Review the actions which you wrote down from Session 2's **Blueprints** that you intend to do. How difficult are these actions for you? When do you find them hardest to do?

Interact As a Couple: 15-20 Minutes

1. Share what was most meaningful to you in Session 2.
2. No one enjoys being told that he or she is being selfish. Your marriage can benefit by knowing how to approach one another when the other mate is being selfish. Wisdom, gentleness and a proper approach can all help bring the selfish one back to a correct perspective. Share a couple of ways your mate could **help you** deal with your selfishness:

    _____

    _____

    (It would be a good idea to get your mate's "permission" before applying these suggestions.)

3. Agree on any action you will take to help one another deal with selfishness.
4. Close your time together by praying for one another.

Remember to bring your calendar for **Make a Date** to the next class session.

SESSION 3

Creating Oneness: Benefits and Principles

OBJECTIVES

You will help your group members nurture oneness in their marriages as you guide them to:

- Discover the benefits of oneness in marriage;
- Identify biblical principles for achieving oneness in marriage; and
- Discuss specific actions which help build oneness.

COMMENTS

1. This session is one of the most positive and crucial in the whole study. People often hear about the problems and failures in marriage. This session explores some of the rich benefits of marriage, and provides practical help for achieving those benefits.
2. You may wish to have extra Bibles for any who did not bring theirs.
3. Again, light refreshments as people arrive help set a tone of friendly anticipation. And name tags are still helpful.
4. If someone joins the group for the first time at this session, be sure to introduce those who do not know each other and assist them in beginning some informal conversation.

Oneness in marriage brings rich benefits to a couple as each person pursues unity instead of selfishly putting individual interests first.

Student is on page 65.

(15-20 Minutes)

Ask for a show of hands of those who completed the HomeBuilders Project from the last session. Do not chide those who did not, but encourage them to complete this week's project and, if needed, make up any unfinished projects. Have two or three people share one result or insight from their project (the purpose of this is for accountability). Congratulate those who did the project, and underscore the importance of doing the project from each session.

Have people form groups of no more than six per group. Then share with the class your answer to the following two questions (which you have lettered on the chalkboard or an overhead transparency). Then have the groups share their answers starting with the person who has worn his or her wedding band for the longest time without taking it off. Limit all answers to 45 seconds or less.

1. **What have you discovered about yourself and your mate?**
2. **What was the most meaningful result of the last session as you worked with your mate to overcome selfishness and isolation?**

Summarize this sharing with this Review statement:

> *"In the first two sessions, you saw that selfishness produces isolation in marriage. Neither is a part of God's plan for marriage—instead, He wants to defeat them. In this session we are going to look at His blueprint for replacing isolation (a natural result) with oneness (a supernatural result)."*

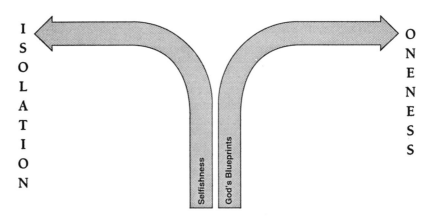

(30-40 Minutes)

Comment: "It is easy to see the benefit of oneness or unity in a physical activity such as a three-legged race or a tug-of-war. Marriage, however, is a very complex relationship, and the effort required to defeat selfishness and achieve oneness may sometimes seem too steep a price to pay. Let's look at a few of the many rich benefits that oneness provides which really do make the process of defeating selfishness more than worthwhile."

Distribute the Session 3 handout. Lead the class in answering the following questions:

A. The Benefits of Oneness
(10 Minutes)

Student is on page 66.

1. What do the following Scriptures teach us about some of the benefits of oneness in a relationship?
   Psalm 133:1

   _____

   Answer: Pleasant...living in unity.

   Ecclesiastes 4:9-12

   _____

   Answer: Helping in labor. Assisting one who falls. Warmth. Strength against adversaries.

2. From your experience, what are some other benefits you gain from being one with your mate?

   _____

   Tip: Divide the group into same-sex pairs. Then have each pair work together in writing a list of other benefits of being one with our mates. Allow about two minutes, then call for volunteers to read aloud items from their lists.

Comment: "Knowing the benefits of oneness leads to an obvious question: How do we achieve it in our marriage? Answering this question is the focus of the next segment."

HOMEBUILDERS PRINCIPLE #2:

Oneness in marriage involves complete unity with each other.

Student is on page 66.

B. Achieving Oneness
(10-15 Minutes)

1. What would society say is the way to achieve oneness in marriage?

_____

Answer: By working hard at your marriage. By improving your sex life. By each of you doing your share in household responsibilities and in working on the relationship (the 50/50 plan).

Tip: Invite volunteers to suggest as many answers as possible to Question 1.

Comment: "At least some of the ideas shared are very positive, helpful suggestions. However, most human plans tend to miss some very important factors."

2. What important factors are missing from most secular instruction in achieving oneness?

_____

Answer: Involving God in a relationship, obedience to God's Word; recognition of selfishness as the root cause of trouble and solving it as a problem. Awareness that only God offers the means to change a selfish nature.

Tip: Invite class members who have not had an opportunity to answer yet to respond to Question 2.

3. In his letter to the church at Philippi, Paul addressed the issue of oneness among Christians. The points he made also show how to achieve oneness within marriage.

   [1] "If therefore there is any encouragement in Christ, if there is any consolation of love, if there is any fellowship of the Spirit, if any affection and compassion,

2 "make my joy complete by being of the same mind, maintaining the same love, united in spirit, intent on one purpose.

3 "Do nothing from selfishness or empty conceit, but with humility of mind let each of you regard one another as more important than himself;

4 "do not merely look out for your own personal interests, but also for the interests of others" (Philippians 2:1-4).

What does Paul say in verses 3 and 4 that relates to what you learned from Sessions 1 and 2 about selfishness?

_____

Answer: Don't act from selfishness, have a humble attitude and put the interests and needs of others ahead of our own.

Tip: Call on a volunteer to read aloud the introductory statement under Item 3. Then ask four other people to each read aloud one verse of Philippians 2:1-4.

4. Share an illustration of a time when you did or did not deny yourself for your mate:

_____

What was the result?

_____

Tip: Briefly share an illustration of one time when you did or did not deny yourself for your mate. Then invite others in the group to tell of a similar incident. Ask the others in the group to tell the results of incidents in their marriage when they did not deny themselves.

Option: If time allows, call attention to verse 1, pointing out that the repeated word "if" is not an expression of doubt, but is a literary device used for emphasis. Other ways of phrasing include "since" or "because" or "obviously there is." Ask, "What does verse 1 indicate about the foundation on which oneness is built?"

5. What does verse 2 say to you about how to achieve oneness in a relationship?

_____

Answer: Be sure the group recognizes the emphasis Paul is placing on oneness by defining it with four distinct phrases: "being of the same mind, maintaining the same love, united in spirit, intent on one purpose."

Comment: "Paul's phrase, 'intent on one purpose,' leads us to examine what God's purpose—or blueprint—for marriage really is. That will be the focus of Session 4."

Option: You may want to share this four-step plan for achieving oneness:
1. *Agree on the goal.*
2. *Deal with any conflict.*
3. *Walk together.*
4. *Build from the same set of blueprints.*

HOMEBUILDERS PRINCIPLE #3:

In order to achieve oneness, a couple must share a strong commitment to God's purpose for marriage.

Student is on page 67.

C. Evaluating Levels of Oneness
(10-15 Minutes)

This section is intended to lead participants to evaluate the level of oneness in their marriages.

Instruct each person to think carefully and then write the answer to the three questions. Before they begin, share your own answer to one of the questions as a sample of how they might proceed. Your willingness to show your imperfections and your desire to grow will encourage others to respond honestly, also. Explain that participants will have the opportunity to share these responses, but no one will be required to do so.

State how much time you will allow (about 10 minutes) and that you will monitor the time so they can keep moving and complete each question.

Work individually to answer these questions to help you evaluate evidence of oneness in your marriage.

1. On a scale of 1-10 (1=lowest; 10=highest), rate the degree that each of these actions (Philippians 2:2) is evident in your marriage. Give one example of each action and write why you chose the rating you did.

"being of the same mind" Example:	1 2 3 4 5 6 7 8 9 10 Why?
"maintaining the same love" Example:	1 2 3 4 5 6 7 8 9 10 Why?
"united in spirit" Example:	1 2 3 4 5 6 7 8 9 10 Why?
"intent on one purpose" Example:	1 2 3 4 5 6 7 8 9 10 Why?

2. What other evidence of oneness have you noticed in your marriage recently?

3. What evidence have you seen in your marriage recently of isolation/selfishness instead of oneness?

Tip: As people work, announce two or three times how much time they have left and approximately how far they should be by this point. Also be available to answer questions in case anyone is uncertain of how to proceed with an item.

Call time and invite volunteers to share one example of oneness from the category which they ranked as highest. Be prepared to begin this sharing yourself.

Student is on page 68.

Make a date with your mate to meet in the next few days to complete *HomeBuilders Project #3*. Your leader will ask at the next session for you to share one thing from this experience.

—————————   —————————   ————————————————————————

Date   Time   Location

Instruct couples to take a moment to agree together on a time this week to complete the HomeBuilders Project. Remind them to keep their completed HomeBuilders handouts to refer to at that time. At the next session you will again ask them to share one experience from this interaction.

Staying Close by Dennis Rainey.

Chapter 11, "God's Purpose for Oneness," expands on the material discussed in this session.

Dismiss in prayer, or invite group members to volunteer one-sentence prayers asking God's help in creating true oneness in marriage. Remind class members to keep the date they set to complete HomeBuilders Project #3.

Invite everyone to enjoy a time of refreshments and fellowship.

Creating Oneness

Oneness in marriage brings rich benefits to a couple as each person pursues unity instead of selfishly putting individual interests first.

1. What have you discovered about yourself and your mate?
2. What was the most meaningful result of the last session as you worked with your mate to overcome selfishness and isolation?

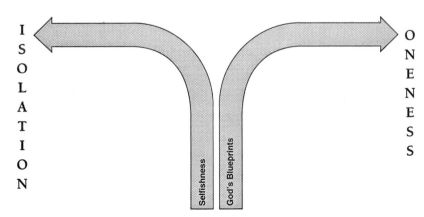

A. The Benefits of Oneness

1. What do the following Scriptures teach us about some of the benefits of oneness in a relationship?

   Psalm 133:1

   _____

   Ecclesiastes 4:9-12

   _____

2. From your experience, what are some other benefits you gain from being one with your mate?

   _____

HOMEBUILDERS PRINCIPLE #2:

Oneness in marriage involves complete unity with each other.

B. Achieving Oneness

1. What would society say is the way to achieve oneness in marriage?

   _____

2. What important factors are missing from most secular instruction in achieving oneness?

   _____

3. In his letter to the church at Philippi, Paul addressed the issue of oneness among Christians. The points he made also show how to achieve oneness within marriage.

   [1] "If therefore there is any encouragement in Christ, if there is any consolation of love, if there is any fellowship of the Spirit, if any affection and compassion,
   [2] "make my joy complete by being of the same mind, maintaining the same love, united in spirit, intent on one purpose.
   [3] "Do nothing from selfishness or empty conceit, but with humility of mind let each of you regard one another as more important than himself;
   [4] "do not merely look out for your own personal interests, but also for the interests of others" (Philippians 2:1-4).

What does Paul say in verses 3 and 4 that relates to what you learned from Sessions 1 and 2 about selfishness?

_____

4.   Share an illustration of a time when you did or did not deny yourself for your mate.

_____

What was the result?

_____

5.   What does verse 2 say to you about how to achieve oneness in a relationship?

_____

The four-step plan for achieving oneness:
1. Agree on the goal.
2. Deal with any conflict.
3. Walk together.
4. Build from the same set of blueprints.

HOMEBUILDERS PRINCIPLE #3:

In order to achieve oneness, a couple must share a strong commitment to God's purpose for marriage.

C. Evaluating Levels of Oneness

Work individually to answer these questions to help you evaluate evidence of oneness in your marriage.

1.   On a scale of 1-10 (1=lowest; 10=highest), rate the degree that each of these actions (Philippians 2:2) is evident in your marriage. Give an example of each action and write why you chose the rating you did.

"being of the same mind" Example:	1 2 3 4 5 6 7 8 9 10 Why?
"maintaining the same love" Example:	1 2 3 4 5 6 7 8 9 10 Why?
"united in spirit" Example:	1 2 3 4 5 6 7 8 9 10 Why?
"intent on one purpose" Example:	1 2 3 4 5 6 7 8 9 10 Why?

2   What other evidence of oneness have you noticed in your marriage recently?

_____

3. What evidence have you seen in your marriage recently of isolation/selfishness instead of oneness?

_____

Make a date with your mate to meet in the next few days to complete **HomeBuilders Project #3**. Your leader will ask at the next session for you to share one thing from this experience.

_____ _____ _____

Date   Time   Location

Staying Close by Dennis Rainey.

Chapter 11, "God's Purpose for Oneness," expands on the material discussed in this session.

HomeBuilders Project #3

Individually: 5-10 Minutes

Answer each of the following questions and prepare to discuss them with your mate.

1. When was a time you felt that you and your mate experienced oneness?
2. What factors contributed to that experience?
3. Which of the Philippians 2:2 principles for experiencing oneness were involved in that experience?
   - being of the same mind
   - maintaining the same love
   - united in spirit
   - intent on one purpose

Interact as a Couple: 15-25 Minutes

1. Review Session 3 and complete any previous sessions and/or projects that are not finished. Discuss those points that stand out in your mind.
2. Compare your responses to the questions about evaluating the level of oneness in your marriage. On which items did you agree? On which did your responses differ?
3. Tell each other your recollections of a time when you experienced oneness in your marriage. Describe what you recall as the factors which contributed to those experiences and the principles from Philippians 2:2 which were involved.
4. What are some actions you will both agree to take in the next few days to help build oneness in your marriage?

Remember to bring your calendar for **Make a Date** to the next class session.

Creating Oneness: God's Purpose for Marriage

OBJECTIVES

You will help your group members continue to nurture oneness in their marriages as you guide them to:

- Identify commitment to God's blueprints as the key to achieving oneness and harmony in marriage;
- Evaluate how God's blueprints for marriage are being followed in their homes; and
- Plan specific ways in which to mirror God's image better in their marriages.

COMMENTS

1. Session 4 explores five central purposes for marriage which are clearly shown in God's Word. As people consider these purposes, and then examine their own expectations for marriage, they will confront their own commitment, or lack of commitment, to God's plans for life and marriage.
2. You may wish to have extra Bibles for any who did not bring theirs.
3. Again, light refreshments as people arrive help set a tone of friendly anticipation, and name tags are still helpful.
4. If someone joins the group for the first time at this session, be sure to introduce those who do not know each other and assist them in beginning some informal conversation. If others return after being gone for a session, welcome them back, keeping the focus on what will happen in this session, rather than on what they missed by being gone.

Oneness in marriage is achieved as both husband and wife yield to God and work together in building their home from the same set of blueprints: the Bible.

(10-15 Minutes)

*As people arrive, engage them in friendly conversation about the events of the past week. Then start on time by briefly sharing one insight you gained from completing **HomeBuilders Project #3.** Then have everyone stand and find out from three different individuals or couples one thing they found meaningful from last week's project. After three or four minutes, invite volunteers to share one insight that another person told about gaining from the project. This type of sharing provides an opportunity to call on someone who has not shared much with the rest of the class. It is often easier to report on what another person said than to share one's own thoughts or feelings. Conclude this warm up by congratulating those who did the project. Emphasize the importance of doing the project from each session.*

(35-45 Minutes)

A. God's Purpose for Marriage
(15-20 Minutes)

Distribute copies of the Session 4 handouts.

Student is on page 77.

1. Match the following Scriptures with God's five purposes for marriage:

    a. Genesis 1:26,27   MANAGE God's Creation

    b. Genesis 1:28a   MODEL Christ's Relationship to His Church

    c. Genesis 1:28b   MIRROR God's Image

    d. Genesis 2:18 &
        1 Corinthians 11:11   MULTIPLY a Godly Heritage

    e. Ephesians 5:31   MUTUALLY Complete One Another

Tip: Ask for a volunteer to read aloud the first Scripture reference (Genesis 1:26,27). Then ask class members to tell which of the purposes for marriage is described there (MIRROR God's Image). Point out that both male and female are included in that declaration. Continue similarly with the other four purposes.

Answer:

a. Genesis 1:26, 27   *MIRROR God's Image (male and female)*

b. Genesis 1:28a   *MULTIPLY a Godly Heritage (be fruitful)*

c. Genesis 1:28b   *MANAGE God's Creation (rule)*

d. Genesis 2:18 &   *MUTUALLY Complete One Another (suitable*
    1 Corinthians 11:11   *helper; not independent)*

e. Ephesians 5:31   *MODEL Christ and Church (united)*

2. Why is each purpose important in a marriage? List ways each can be applied in your marriage today.

_____

Tip: Instruct class members to form at least five groups of no more than six persons per group. Then assign each group one of the five purposes for marriage. Group mem-

bers are to list as many ways that they can think of as to why their assigned purpose is important in a marriage. Allow three or four minutes for groups to work. Then call time, and invite a representative from each group to share their list. Be prepared to add the following points should they be overlooked by the groups:

Answer:

> *MIRROR God's Image: Both male and female were created in God's image. Both have equal dignity and with it equal responsibility to live as God's person in the home and community.*
> *MULTIPLY a Godly Heritage: Marriage is not just for the benefit of the couple, but is to produce others who reflect God in the world.*
> *MANAGE God's Creation: All that a couple does should be evaluated in light of the responsibility of being good stewards of all God has provided.*
> *MUTUALLY Complete One Another: Each person is incomplete; marriage is God's best means for filling the gaps as each person is made whole by meeting the needs of the other.*
> MODEL Christ and the Church: The unselfish love of a husband and the willing submission of a wife is a living example of the relationship between Christ and His church.

HOMEBUILDERS PRINCIPLE #4:

When we yield to God and build together from His blueprints, we begin the process of experiencing oneness.

Student is on page 78.

B. Evaluating How I Mirror God's Image
(20-25 Minutes)

This segment helps people evaluate how they are doing in mirroring God's image in various areas of their lives. This awareness is intended to lead people to identify at least one specific way in which they can grow in fulfilling God's purpose for their marriages.

> *Refer participants to the evaluation section of the Blueprints handout. Instruct each person to complete the three items in the section. State how much time you will allow (at least eight minutes) and that you will monitor the time so they can keep moving and complete all three items. They will want to go back to some of the items when they complete HomeBuilders Project #4 later in the week for a more thorough consideration. Explain that you will ask each person to share one item from this section. Before they begin work, share your own completion of one line on the chart as a sample of how they might proceed with the first item. Be willing to show your imperfections and your desire to grow so that others may feel able to respond honestly to these probing questions.*

Let's consider one of the purposes for marriage:

1. How well is my marriage mirroring God's image—representing Him—in the areas and relationships listed in the following chart? *Rate your marriage on a scale of 1 (lowest) to 10 (highest) in how you and your mate reflect God to these people:*

We mirror God's:	to each other	to our children	to our neighbors	to coworkers
...perfect love for imperfect people;				
...loving-kindness, by serving to meet needs;				
...commitment by patient support;				
...peace, by resolving conflicts.				

2. Are there any hindrances to my mirroring God's image in my marriage? What needs to be done to remove any barriers?

   _____

3. What did I learn about my marriage from this evaluation?

   _____

Tip: As people work, announce two or three times how much time they have left and approximately how far they should be by this point. Also be available to answer questions in case anyone is uncertain of how to proceed with an item.

Call time and invite each person to share his or her answer to one item they discussed. You may want to begin the sharing yourself. If you have more than ten people in the class, divide into groups of at least five people per group in order to do this sharing. Remind people that the purpose of the sharing is to help each other think of ideas and actions beyond those each person might come up with on their own. However, it is perfectly acceptable for a person to "pass" on sharing at any time.

Student is on page 79.

Make a date with your mate to meet in the next few days to complete *HomeBuilders Project #4*. Your leader will ask at the next session for you to share one thing from this experience.

Date	Time	Location

*Have group members look at the **Make a Date** section and take a moment for participants to agree with their mates on a time this week to complete the **HomeBuilders Project**. Remind them to save their completed **Blueprints** page to refer to at that time. Also, at the next session you will again ask them to share one experience from this interaction.*

Staying Close by Dennis Rainey.

Chapters 11 and 12—"God's Purpose for Oneness" and "The Master Plan for Oneness"—expand on the material discussed in this session.

Dismiss in prayer, or invite group members to volunteer one-sentence prayers asking God's help in creating true oneness in marriage.

Invite everyone to enjoy a time of refreshments and fellowship.

God's Purpose for Marriage

Oneness in marriage is achieved as both husband and wife yield to God and work together in building their home from the same set of blueprints: the Bible.

A. God's Purpose for Marriage

1. Match the following Scriptures with God's five purposes for marriage:
   a. Genesis 1:26,27   MANAGE God's Creation
   b. Genesis 1:28a   MODEL Christ's Relationship to His Church
   c. Genesis 1:28b   MIRROR God's Image
   d. Genesis 2:18 and   MULTIPLY a Godly Heritage
      1 Corinthians 11:11
   e. Ephesians 5:31   MUTUALLY Complete One Another

2.   Why is each purpose important in a marriage? List ways each can be applied in your marriage today.

_____

HOMEBUILDERS PRINCIPLE #4:

When we yield to God and build together from His blueprints, we begin the process of experiencing oneness.

B. Evaluating How I Mirror God's Image

Let's consider one of the purposes for marriage:

1.   How well is my marriage mirroring God's image—representing Him—in the areas and relationships listed below? Rate your marriage on a scale of 1 (lowest) to 10 (highest) in how you and your mate reflect God to these people:

We mirror God's:	to each other	to our children	to our neighbors	to coworkers
...perfect love for imperfect people;				
...loving-kindness, by serving to meet needs;				
...commitment by patient support;				
...peace, by resolving conflicts.				

2.   Are there any hindrances to my mirroring God's image in my marriage? What needs to be done to remove any barriers?

_____

3.   What did I learn about my marriage from this evaluation?

_____

Make a date with your mate to meet in the next few days to complete **HomeBuilders Project #4**. Your leader will ask at the next session for you to share one thing from this experience.

Date	Time	Location

Staying Close by Dennis Rainey.

Chapters 11 and 12—"God's Purpose for Oneness" and "The Master Plan for Oneness"—expand on the material discussed in this session

HomeBuilders Project #4

As a Couple: 5-10 Minutes

1. Review Session 4 and complete any previous sessions and/or projects that are not finished. Discuss those points that stand out in your mind.

2. Compare your responses to the evaluation of how your marriage is mirroring the image. On which points did you agree? On which ones did you give differing responses?

Individually: 15-20 Minutes

Answer each of the following questions and prepare to discuss them with your mate.

1. What would our closest friends say is the purpose of our marriage?

2. In which of God's purposes are we succeeding? (Manage, model, mirror, multiply, mutually complete.)

3. Which ones need work in our marriage? In what way?

4. What hinders our success in accomplishing these purposes?

5. What tough decisions need to be made **now**? In the next 6 to 12 months?

6. What one step could we take this week to move toward fulfilling one of God's purposes in our marriage?

Interact as a Couple: 25-30 Minutes

Discuss with your mate your reflections on and discoveries from the above questions. Please be sure to **agree** on any action step and **how** it will be implemented. Close your time together by praying for one another and for your success in fulfilling God's purposes for your marriage.

Remember to bring your calendar for **Make a Date** to the next class session.

Receiving Your Mate: Recognizing Your Need

OBJECTIVES

You will help your group members nurture oneness in their marriages as you guide them to:

- Identify the ways Adam needed Eve and compare those with ways they need their mates; and
- Discuss the importance and the basis of receiving their mates as God's perfect provision.

COMMENTS

The **Warm Up** questions are important not only to remind people of earlier content, but to keep building a sense of mutual accountability. If your group members merely come to class and do not build a commitment to follow through with genuine growth efforts, they will gain little from this study.

Oneness in marriage requires receiving your mate as God's perfect provision for your needs.

*Student is on
page 87.*

(10-15 Minutes)

*This **Warm Up** section builds on the mutual trust and concern that has been built in your group during the first four sessions. The question encourages people to reveal a little more of themselves, helping them develop honest and open responses to the questions that follow.*

> *Option: On the chalkboard or an overhead transparency, letter the two **Warm Up** questions. Because some people feel uncomfortable sharing in a mixed group, you may want to have people discuss the two questions in small groups separated by gender. Smaller groups will also allow more people to share within the time available. If you do break up into small groups, and if time allows, have volunteers share an answer to one item when the groups come back together.*

1. One thing I *would not* want to change about my mate is...

    _____

2. Share your answer to one of these questions from *HomeBuilders Project #4*:
    ❑ What would your closest friends say is the purpose of your marriage?

    _____

    ❑ What one step did you take since our last session toward fulfilling one of God's purposes in your marriage?

    _____

> *Tip: Ask for a show of hands of those who completed **HomeBuilders Project #4**. Commend those who did it and stress the long-term value of regularly setting aside time with our mates to talk about our relationships. Share your answer to one of the two **HomeBuilders Project** questions, then ask your class members to share their answers to one of the questions.*

We have seen that selfishness produces isolation in marriage, while following God's blueprints leads to oneness. Now we will explore the importance of receiving one's mate as God's special gift for our aloneness needs.

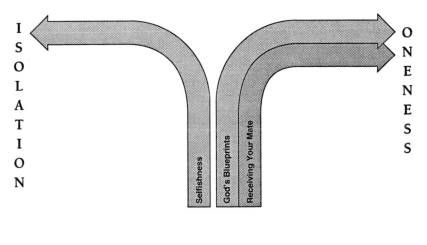

(35-45 Minutes)

The Blueprints section explores a key principle: The joy of God's provision. Many couples do not understand this principle and thereby miss out on it. The personal nature of some of these questions makes it easier for some people to share in smaller groups than with the whole class. Thus, if you have more than ten people in the class, divide them into groups of at least five people per group.

Distribute copies of the Session 5 handouts you have duplicated.

In Genesis 2:18-23, we find the familiar story of Adam and Eve. Our familiarity with Scriptures such as this can blind us to profound insights—insights that, when applied, can strengthen every marriage. Let's look at what we can learn from this passage to help us achieve oneness in marriage.

A. Everyone's Need
(10-15 Minutes)

1. Read Genesis 2:18-23. What need did God build into Adam that was not filled by God's personal presence? What was "not good" about Adam as God created him?

_____

Answer: Adam needed a mate, a companion, "a helper suitable for him" or "corresponding to him." "Alone" in this context is obviously a negative situation, since God specifically said it was "not good" and took action to remedy the problem.

Student is on page 88.

Tip: To help your group members focus on what was negative in the situation, you may want to ask a follow-up question such as, "What is another word for being alone?" (Isolation)

2. What are some likely reasons God made Adam incomplete?

   _____

   Answer: To keep him from feeling self-sufficient. To enable him to recognize his need of God and of his mate, so that his mate would be able to provide for areas in which he lacked.

3. Identify two or three ways you are incomplete and need your mate.

   _____

   Tip: Your group members may not be accustomed to thinking of themselves as lacking something which their mates provide. To get them started, share some ways that you are incomplete without your mate. Then ask each person to work privately on their written answers and be ready to share one answer.

Student is on page 88.

B. Awareness of Need
(15-20 Minutes)

1. Reread Genesis 2:19,20. What did naming animals have to do with Adam's aloneness? How aware of being alone do you think Adam was before he named the animals?

   _____

   Answer: Adam recognized that he did not have a suitable companion. There is no evidence Adam had any awareness of his need before then.

2. Why did God want Adam to see his need for a mate?

   _____

   Answer: Until Adam recognized his need, he would never adequately appreciate God or God's provision, Eve.

   Comment: "It may be fun to speculate about what went on in Adam's head, but we must not lose sight of what God was trying to do."

3. What are some ways you see your need for your mate today that you did not recognize when you first got married?

   _____

4. How do you think your awareness of needing your mate may change in the next five years?

_____

Tip: If responses are slow in coming, ask, "If things continue as they are now, do you think in five years you will be more aware of your need for your mate or less aware?" You might suggest this as a question for couples to refer back to while working on the HomeBuilders Project this week.

5. At the beginning of your relationship with your mate, how aware was God of all your needs (past, present and future)?

_____

Answer: He was completely aware of your needs. Your mate is God's provision for your needs.

Note: This is a key point for couples to digest. Many married couples end up spending so much time focusing on their mates' shortcomings that they forget how much they need their mates. And the thought that God actually gave their mates to them to meet their needs may strike some couples as incredible.

If you sense that people don't grasp the significance of this fact, you might turn to your mate and say something like, "God gave me this person in order to meet my needs. She is God's provision for me." Invite participants to consider the fact that a similar declaration is true for them.

C. My Mate Needs Me
(10 Minutes)

Student is on page 89.

Individually, list ways you see your mate needing you. (Try to list 10 if time permits.) You will share this list with your mate during the *HomeBuilders Project* this week.

_____

Tip: At the end of the allotted time, ask each person to share one item from his or her list, either within their small group or with the entire class. Again, remind people that such sharing can help stimulate a variety of good ideas, but no one is required to share.

Student is on page 89.

Make a Date

Make a date with your mate to meet in the next few days to complete *HomeBuilders Project #5*. This time for the two of you is as important as the time for the sessions. Your leader will ask at the next session for you to share one thing from this experience.

_____ _____ _____
Date   Time   Location

Tip: Remind couples to set and keep their dates to complete HomeBuilders Project #5. Stress its value in making the truth of the session practical in their relationships.

Recommended Reading

Tip: Call attention to the Recommended Reading.

Building Your Mate's Self-Esteem by Dennis and Barbara Rainey.

Accepting your mate is one of the cornerstones of a godly marriage. This book can help you express your acceptance and belief in each other. An intensely practical book, it will teach you how to deal with the haunting problems of the past, how to give your mate the freedom to fail and how to help your mate be liberated from questions of self-doubt.

Staying Close by Dennis Rainey.

Chapters 5-7 will help you further consider the issues discussed in this session.

Conclude with a brief time of prayer. Invite volunteers to pray aloud, thanking God for his/her mate.

Invite everyone to enjoy a time of refreshments and fellowship.

SESSION 5

Receiving Your Mate: Recognizing Your Need

Oneness in marriage requires receiving your mate as God's perfect provision for your needs.

1. One thing I **would not** want to change about my mate is...

_____

2. Share your answer to one of these questions from **HomeBuilders Project #4**:
    ❑ What would your closest friends say is the purpose of your marriage?

_____

    ❑ What one step did you take since our last session toward fulfilling one of God's purposes in your marriage?

_____

We have seen that selfishness produces isolation in marriage, while following God's blueprints leads to oneness. Now we will explore the importance of receiving one's mate as God's special gift for our aloneness needs.

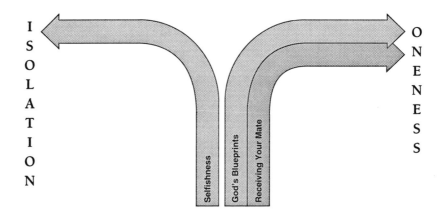

In Genesis 2:18-23, we find the familiar story of Adam and Eve. Our familiarity with Scriptures such as this can blind us to profound insights—insights that, when applied, can strengthen every marriage. Let's look at what we can learn from this passage to help us achieve oneness in marriage:

A. Everyone's Need

1. Read Genesis 2:18-23. What need did God build into Adam that was not filled by God's personal presence? What was "not good" about Adam as God created him?

    _____

2. What are some likely reasons God made Adam incomplete?

    _____

3. Identify two or three ways you are incomplete and need your mate.

    _____

B. Awareness of Need

1. Reread Genesis 2:19,20. What did naming animals have to do with Adam's aloneness? How aware of being alone do you think Adam was before he named the animals?

    _____

2. Why did God want Adam to see his need for a mate?

    _____

3 What are some ways you see your need for your mate today that you did not recognize when you first got married?

_____

4. How do you think your awareness of needing your mate may change in the next five years?

_____

5. At the beginning of your relationship with your mate, how aware was God of all your needs (past, present and future)?

_____

C. My Mate Needs Me

Individually, list ways you see your mate needing you. (Try to list 10 if time permits.) You will share this list with your mate during the **HomeBuilders Project** this week.

_____

Make a date with your mate to meet in the next few days to complete **HomeBuilders Project #5**. This time for the two of you is as important as the time for the sessions. Your leader will ask at the next session for you to share one thing from this experience.

_____   _____   _____

Date   Time   Location

Building Your Mate's Self-Esteem by Dennis and Barbara Rainey.

Accepting your mate is one of the cornerstones of a godly marriage. This book can help you express your acceptance and belief in each other. An intensely practical book, it will teach you how to deal with the haunting problems of the past, how to give your mate the freedom to fail and how to help your mate be liberated from questions of self-doubt.
Staying Close by Dennis Rainey.

Chapters 5-7 will help you further consider the issues discussed in this session.

HomeBuilders Project #5

As a Couple: 5-10 Minutes

Review the concepts studied in Session 5. Share what really impressed you in the study. Go back over any sections you wanted to discuss with your mate but were unable to.

Individually: 10-15 Minutes

1. Do an inventory of the ways your mate is meeting your needs. Try to list 25 or more if you can. (List on a separate sheet of paper.)
2. Identify which of those are the five most important ways you need him or her.

Interact as a Couple: 10 Minutes

1. Share the results of your inventory with your mate.
2. Affirm (or reaffirm) to your mate your acceptance of him or her as God's perfect provision for your needs.
3. Close your time together in prayer, thanking God for one another.

Remember to bring your calendar for **Make a Date** to the next class session.

SESSION 6

Receiving Your Mate: God's Perfect Provision

OBJECTIVES

You will help your group members nurture oneness in their marriages as you guide them to:

- Analyze how weaknesses in mates have an impact on receiving them as God's provision; and
- Affirm specific ways they and their mates need each other and can accept one another as God's gift.

COMMENTS

By this sixth session your group members should have come to know one another well enough to feel somewhat relaxed and comfortable in talking with each other—at least about external aspects of their marriages. This session probes some very sensitive areas, exploring ways that we need our mates. Some people may have difficulty admitting these ways to themselves or to their mates, let alone to other people. Your role here, providing acceptance and support without pressing anyone, is crucial. Pray for sensitivity to each person as a unique being. Remind people that they can pass on any question they prefer not to answer.

Oneness in marriage requires receiving your mate, regardless of his or her imperfections, as God's perfect provision for your needs.

Student is on page 99.

(10-15 Minutes)

*This **Warm Up** section assumes people in your class are no longer threatened by sharing some of the ups and downs of their marriages. Even those who are the most reticent will enjoy the opportunity to "brag" a little on the strengths their mates possess.*

Distribute 4x6-inch index cards or sheets of blank paper on which people can write their answers to this question.

Option: Because smaller groups allow more people to share within the time available, divide into two or more small groups in which each person responds to this question.

What are your mate's three greatest strengths—and how do they complement your own strengths and weaknesses? (Question taken from *The Questions Book for Marriage Intimacy* by Dennis and Barbara Rainey. Published by FamilyLife, 1988.)

Tip: Tell the group about your own mate's greatest strengths and how you feel they complement your strengths and weaknesses. Then ask each person to share his or her response to the same question.

*Tip: After everyone has had opportunity to "brag," ask for a show of hands of those who completed **HomeBuilders Project #5**. Share from your own list several of the* *ways your mate meets your needs, then ask for volunteers to share one or two ways their mates meet their needs.*

We have seen that oneness is enhanced as we receive our mates as God's special gift for our aloneness needs. However, we sometimes allow barriers to keep us from doing that, resulting in dissatisfaction and isolation.

(35-45 Minutes)

The Blueprints section helps each individual recognize areas of personal need and accept his or her mate as God's provision for those needs.

   Distribute copies of the Session 6 handouts you have duplicated.

In Session 5, we examined Genesis 2:18-20, where God determined that it is not good for man to be alone. Let's look at the next few verses to see what we can learn to help us achieve oneness in marriage.

A. God's Provision for Our Need
(10-15 minutes)

Student is on page 100.

1. Read Genesis 2:21,22. List five things God did in these two verses:

   a. _____   b. _____
   c. _____   d. _____
   e. _____

   Answer: Caused Adam to sleep, took a rib, closed the flesh, made a woman and brought her to Adam.

2. Which of these actions seems most significant to you? Why?

   _____

Student is on page 100.

B. Our Response to God's Provision
(10-15 Minutes)

1. Read Genesis 2:23. What had Eve done up to this point to warrant Adam's acceptance?

    _____

    Answer: Other than obviously looking better to Adam than any of the animals he had been naming, she had done nothing. Nor had he done anything to earn acceptance from her.

2. Why was Adam able to immediately recognize Eve as the mate who would fulfill his need?

    _____

    Answer: We can assume there was an immediate attraction between them. However, the only clue given in the passage is that Adam must have recognized that God was presenting her as a gift from Himself. And Eve knew that God had specifically brought her to Adam.

3. Who did Adam know better—Eve or God? _____

    Answer: Obviously, God. Why is this important? Although Adam did not yet know Eve, he did know God and trusted Him.

4. Are you more a student of:

    ❑ your mate (strengths, weaknesses, etc.)
    OR
    ❑ the One who provided him/her for you?

    Comment: "This passage clarifies two important concepts:
    - *No married person is complete until he/she is united with his/her God-given counterpart. Many individuals struggle within their marriage because they are unaware of their need of their mate.*
    - *Acceptance of our mates as God's provision for our needs frees the relationship from the pressure which results when acceptance is based on performance. Just as Eve did nothing to earn Adam's acceptance, we do not have to perform or satisfy someone's list of conditions. And like Adam, we need to receive our mates simply on the basis of Who gave him/her to us."*

HOMEBUILDERS PRINCIPLE #5:

The basis for my acceptance of my mate is faith in God's character and trustworthiness.

5.   What causes us to reject rather than receive our mates?

_____

Tip: Encourage people to think of specific incidents in which they reacted with rejection rather than acceptance.

Comment: Summarize the ideas shared with this comment: "We tend to focus on our mates and lose our focus on God. And when we are focused on our mates, it is usually easier to notice flaws than strengths."

6.   Since God provided your mate, can you reject your mate without rejecting God? Why?

_____

Answer: No. Rejection of the gift is rejection of the Giver.

Tip: If you have non-Christians in the group or people who were not Christians when they married, ask the group to suggest an answer for someone who says, "But when we were married, neither of us even knew God, let alone trusted Him. How could my mate be God's gift to me under that circumstance?" (The Scriptures clearly show that God is sovereign in the affairs of individuals and nations. Have the group look at Romans 8:28 to see the most common way God demonstrates His sovereignty: He shows His authority by turning even what is done in rebellion against Him into results that achieve His purposes. See Genesis 50:20.)

Tip: If the issue of spouse abuse is raised, call attention to these Scriptures that provide wise counsel:

- *Romans 13:1 and 1 Peter 2:13-15 teach God's establishment of governmental authority to control those who do wrong. A person in danger should not hesitate to contact the authorities for protection.*
- *Romans 5:8 shares Christ's example of loving the sinner even though hating sin (Psalm 45:7). One spouse's wrong acts do not excuse retaliation by the other.*
- *Proverbs 14:7 says to "leave the presence of a fool." This does not mean divorce; it simply advises establishing enough space to avoid the influence of the fool.*

7. Consider the results of not receiving your mate. Describe such a marriage 10 to 20 years from now.

_____

Tip: After several responses have been shared, ask "What do these predictions say to you about receiving your mate as God's best provision for your needs?"

8. Which of these statements could you most readily apply in your marriage? Weaknesses in my mate are...

❏ a. opportunities for me to be needed.

❏ b. tools of God to cause me to trust Him.

❏ c. only changed through a climate of loving acceptance.

Tip: Ask for a show of hands of those who chose the first statement. Do the same for the other two. Then invite someone who marked the statement most commonly chosen to explain why he or she feels that idea is significant. After two or three have commented, do the same for the other two statements. If no one chooses a particular statement, share your own thoughts on its importance.

HOMEBUILDERS PRINCIPLE #6:

A godly marriage *is not* created by finding a perfect, flawless person, but *is* created by allowing God's perfect love and acceptance to flow through one imperfect person—you—toward another imperfect person—your mate.

Student is on page 101.

Make a date with your mate to meet in the next few days to complete *HomeBuilders Project #6*. This time for the two of you is as important as the time for the sessions. Your leader will ask at the next session for you to share one thing from this experience.

_____   _____   _____
     Date   Time   Location

Remind couples to set and keep their dates to complete HomeBuilders Project #6. Stress its value in making the truth of the session practical in their relationships.

Call attention to the Recommended Reading.

Staying Close by Dennis Rainey.
    Chapters 5-7 will help you consider further the issues discussed in this session.

Conclude with a time of prayer in small groups. Then invite everyone to enjoy a time of refreshments and fellowship.

SESSION 6

Receiving Your Mate: God's Perfect Provision

Oneness in marriage requires receiving your mate, regardless of his or her imperfections, as God's perfect provision for your needs.

What are your mate's three greatest strengths—and how do they complement your own strengths and weaknesses? (Question taken from *The Questions Book for Marriage Intimacy* by Dennis and Barbara Rainey. Published by FamilyLife, 1988.)

We have seen that oneness is enhanced as we receive our mates as God's special gift for our aloneness needs. However, we sometimes allow barriers to keep us from doing that, resulting in dissatisfaction and isolation.

Blueprints

In Session 5, we examined Genesis 2:18-20, where God determined that it is not good for man to be alone. Let's look at the next few verses to see what we can learn to help us achieve oneness in marriage.

A. God's Provision for Our Need (Genesis 2:21,22)

1. Read Genesis 2:21,22. List five things God did in these two verses:

   a. _____ b. _____

   c. _____ d. _____

   e. _____

2. Which of these actions seems most significant to you? Why?

   _____

   _____

B. Our Response to God's Provision (Genesis 2:23)

1. Read Genesis 2:23. What had Eve done up to this point to warrant Adam's acceptance?

   _____

2. Why was Adam able to immediately recognize Eve as the mate who would fulfill his need?

   _____

3. Who did Adam know better—Eve or God? _____

4. Are you more a student of:

   ❑ your mate (strengths, weaknesses, etc.)

   OR

   ❑ the One who provided him/her for you?

HomeBuilders Principle #5:

The basis for my acceptance of my mate is faith in God's character and trustworthiness.

5. What causes us to reject rather than receive our mates?

   _____

6. Since God provided your mate, can you reject your mate without rejecting God? Why?

    _____

7. Consider the results of not receiving your mate. Describe such a marriage 10 to 20 years from now.

    _____

8. Which of these statements could you most readily apply in your marriage? Weaknesses in my mate are...

    ❑ a. opportunities for me to be needed.
    ❑ b. tools of God to cause me to trust Him.
    ❑ c. only changed through a climate of loving acceptance.

HOMEBUILDERS PRINCIPLE #6:

A godly marriage *is not* created by finding a perfect, flawless person, but *is* created by allowing God's perfect love and acceptance to flow through one imperfect person—you—toward another imperfect person—your mate.

Make a date with your mate to meet in the next few days to complete **HomeBuilders Project #6**. This time for the two of you is as important as the time for the sessions. Your leader will ask at the next session for you to share one thing from this experience.

_____   _____   _____
Date   Time   Location

Staying Close by Dennis Rainey.
    Chapters 5-7 will help you consider further the issues discussed in this session.

Individually: 10 Minutes

Spend time in prayer:

1. Confess to God as sin any rejection of, withdrawal from, or bitterness toward your mate. Thank God for His forgiveness and the cleansing blood of Christ.

   "If we confess our sins, He is faithful and righteous to forgive us our sins and to cleanse us from all unrighteousness" (1 John 1:9).

2. Commit to God, by faith, to receive your mate based upon the integrity and sovereignty of God. Be sure to add this commitment to your love letter.

3. Commit to God to trust Him with your mate's weaknesses and to love your mate unconditionally with Christ's love (apart from performance). Be certain you put this commitment in your love letter.

4. Write out the answers to the following questions in the form of a love letter to give to your mate.
   a. What were the qualities that attracted me the most to you when we first met?
   b. Do I see and accept you as you really are? What have I not accepted in you?
   c. Do you see and accept me as I really am? In what areas do I feel that you have not accepted me? How does this make me feel?

Interact as a Couple: 15-20 Minutes

1. Share and discuss your letters.
2. Tell your mate the commitment you made to God during your individual prayer time.
3. Affirm (or reaffirm) to your mate your acceptance of him or her as God's perfect provision for your needs.
4. Close your time together by taking turns thanking God for each other.

Remember to bring your calendar for **Make a Date** to the next class session.

SESSION 7

Constructing a Relationship: Leave and Cleave

OBJECTIVES

You will help your group members construct a distinctively Christian marriage as you guide them to:

- Define the importance of leaving their own parents, and
- Evaluate the ways in which they are currently cleaving to their mates.

COMMENTS

You may need to monitor time carefully in this session because each part of the **Blueprints** section can generate a great deal of interesting interaction. If the group seems intent on staying with a section longer than your time allotment, point out that part of the purpose of the session is to raise issues for couples to discuss further at home. Avoid making frequent references to time limitations, but keep the group aware that the point they are dissecting is best understood in light of the total set of truths being dealt with in the session.

The process of becoming one requires that a couple construct their marriage by leaving parents and cleaving to each other.

Student is on page 109.

(10-15 Minutes)

1. What was one of the first difficult challenges in your commitment to each other that you faced in the early years of your marriage?
2. How did that challenge affect your commitment to each other?

Tip: Letter the above questions on the chalkboard, a blank overhead transparency, or a poster. To encourage openness in sharing answers to these questions, and to allow for more sharing within the available time, consider having the men and women meet in separate small groups (no more than four or five per group). To add a dimension of fun, and if time allows, when the groups complete their sharing and meet back together, check on their stories. Find out whether any couples both told of the same challenge, and if so, whether their views on it varied in any way.

Ask each person to reflect on the HomeBuilders Project #6. Ask for a show of hands of those who did the project. Do not chide those who did not, but encourage them to complete it and, if needed, make up unfinished projects. Have two people share one result of their projects (the purpose of this is accountability). Congratulate those who did and underscore the importance of doing the project for each session.

In Sessions 5 and 6 we saw that with our confidence in God's character and trustworthiness, we can totally accept and receive our mates as His provision for our needs. Many couples today have yet to realize that they have not been following the biblical blueprints for becoming one. God's blueprints for the lifelong process of constructing a godly marriage have three practical phases. We will explore the first two phases in this session, and the third phase in Session 8.

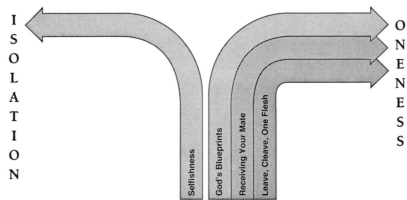

(35-45 Minutes)

Comment: "This session explores two of the three phases in the construction of a Christian marriage. One of the most common errors is assuming that each phase has already been fulfilled. Far too many people think that the command to leave parents (Phase 1), cleave together (Phase 2) and become one flesh (Phase 3) is aimed at new-lyweds. This study will show that each phase must be a lifelong process in order for a couple to achieve and maintain a relationship of openness and trust."

Tip: Distribute copies of the Session 7 handouts you have duplicated. Lead the class in answering the questions on the page.

A. Phase 1—Leave
(10-15 Minutes)

Student is on page 110.

1. Read Genesis 2:24. Once a couple has received each other as God's gift, they must leave their parents. What factors are involved in "leaving" one's parents? How do people establish and maintain independence from parents?

   _____

   Answer: Leaving involves physical, emotional and financial separation, transferring dependence from parents to mate.

   NOTE: The Hebrew term translated "leave" means "to loosen," "to relinquish," or "to forsake."

2. What are some ways couples do not leave their parents?

   _____

   Answer: Continuing to receive financial help. Asking parents to resolve conflicts. Frequently visiting or calling parents. Putting parents' needs ahead of those of mate. Seeking parental advice or approval in place of mate's.

3.   What can happen in a marriage when:
     a. parents are "too clingy"?

_____

Answer: The child may not mature. The spouse may develop resentments which create conflicts.

     b. the son/daughter is dependent on parents and not on his/her mate?

_____

Answer: Mate is not allowed to meet spouse's needs, thwarting oneness in the relationship.

Comment: "It's important for us to keep in mind that no longer being dependent on parents does not mean not having a relationship with them. For example, a couple may borrow money from parents. This transaction would not indicate undue dependence on parents if it is handled in a businesslike manner with an agreed-upon plan for repayment which is fully honored. Nor would parental help in a crisis necessarily indicate excessive dependence. But a pattern of going to parents for repeated assistance is a serious danger signal."

4.   Read Ephesians 6:2,3. What are some practical ways of honoring your parents and providing for them without becoming dependent on them?

_____

Answer: Pray for your parents. Write and call them regularly. Organize special events to honor them. Put together a special written tribute to your parents. Care for them when your help is needed.

Option: If any couples in your group have parents who are now elderly and becoming incapable of caring for themselves, ask "How can a couple balance responsibilities to each other with the needs of aging parents?"

5.   Are there ways you and your mate have not left your parents? How?

_____

6.   What practical advice would you give to:
     a. the dependent son/daughter?

_____

     b. the son/daughter whose parents are "too clingy"?

_____

Student is on page 111.

Tip: Call on someone who has not spoken aloud for a while to offer a suggestion in response to Question 6a. Then invite several others to add further suggestions. Repeat the process with Question 6b.

B. Phase 2—Cleave
(10-15 Minutes)

Tip: Invite a class member to read aloud Genesis 2:24 before you ask Questions 1 and 2.

1. Reread Genesis 2:24. What does the phrase "cleave to his wife" mean in this verse?

   _____

   Answer: The term conveys the sense of strong emotional attachments, a bonding. The Hebrew term for "cleave" involves the idea of clinging, adhering, being united. Cleaving involves a commitment—a promise, guarantee, assurance—to one another, and so involves an act of the will, a conscious decision to form a permanent bond. Thus, cleaving is both a one-time decision and an ongoing process which must be continually reaffirmed.

2. What is the relationship between leaving your parents and cleaving to your mate?

   _____

   Answer: A couple cannot fully cleave to each other until they have truly left their parents. Also, the decision to leave parents cannot be maintained unless the couple continues to cleave to one another.

3. What factors in society and in marriage make cleaving difficult?

   _____

   Answer: If people run out of ideas, ask them to think of factors within an individual (pride, selfishness, etc.), factors between partners (poor communication, competition, etc.) and factors outside the couple (job pressures, in-laws, finances, etc.).

4. Malachi 2:15,16 says "'Take heed then, to your spirit, and let no one deal treacherously against the wife of your youth. For I hate divorce,' says the Lord." Why is cleaving so important to God?

   _____

   Answer: Divorce, the end result of failure to cleave, is one of the few things in the Bible which God specifically says He hates. He feels this way because He created us with a need for oneness that can only be met by the cleaving of marriage. He planned marriage to accomplish purposes which are of great value to Him (we discussed these in Session 2) and He wants us to experience what is best.

5. What are some reasons commitment is important to a marriage relationship? Why is your mate's commitment important to you?

_____

Answer: Commitment is the only way to provide a person with the freedom to be real without fear of rejection.

Student is on page 111.

Make a date with your mate to meet in the next few days to complete *HomeBuilders Project #7*. Your leader will ask at the next session for you to share one thing from this experience.

_____   _____   _____

Date   Time   Location

The Questions Book for Marriage Intimacy by Dennis and Barbara Rainey.

This short book offers 31 questions you've probably never thought to ask your mate. These questions will ignite your curiosity and rekindle your fascination for each other. These questions will spark many memorable hours of sharing, sharpen your understanding of your mate and stimulate closeness in new areas of your marriage.

Refer to the Recommended Reading and HomeBuilders Project #7. Point out that two separate projects are provided, again allowing a couple to focus on one of the phases of constructing a marriage. Suggest that if a couple feels they have unresolved issues remaining from the evaluation exercise during class, they should tackle the same phase in their HomeBuilders Project. However, if they feel satisfied with their responses to that phase, it may be best to explore the other phase during the week. Explain that this week's project may take about ten minutes longer than most others.

Dismiss with a time of prayer, followed by refreshments and fellowship. Remember to be fair with your class by ending on time, even if some of the content cannot be fully covered.

SESSION 7

Constructing a Relationship: Leave and Cleave

The process of becoming one requires that a couple construct their marriage by leaving parents and cleaving to each other.

1. What was one of the first difficult challenges in your commitment to each other that you faced in the early years of your marriage?

2. How did that challenge affect your commitment to each other?

In Sessions 5 and 6 we saw that with our confidence in God's character and trustworthiness, we can totally accept and receive our mates as His provision for our needs. Many couples today have yet to realize that they have not been following the biblical blueprints for becoming one. God's blueprints for the lifelong process of constructing a godly marriage have three practical phases. We will explore the first two phases in this session, and the third phase in Session 8.

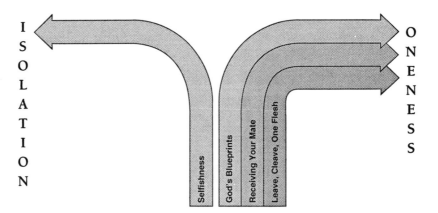

A. Phase 1—Leave

1. Read Genesis 2:24. Once a couple has received each other as God's gift (Genesis 2:18-23), they must leave their parents. What factors are involved in "leaving" one's parents? How do people establish and maintain independence from parents?

   _____

2. What are some ways couples do not leave their parents?

   _____

3. What can happen in a marriage when:
   a. parents are "too clingy"?

   _____

   b. the son/daughter is dependent on parents and not on his/her mate?

   _____

4. Read Ephesians 6:2,3. What are some practical ways of honoring your parents and providing for them without becoming dependent on them?

   _____

5. Are there ways you and your mate have not left your parents? How?

   _____

6. What practical advice would you give to:
   a. the dependent son/daughter?

   _____

b. the son/daughter whose parents are "too clingy"?

B. Phase 2—Cleave

1. Reread Genesis 2:24. What does the phrase "cleave to his wife" mean in this verse?

2. What is the relationship between leaving your parents and cleaving to your mate?

3. What factors in society and in marriage make cleaving difficult?

4. Malachi 2:15,16 says "'Take heed then, to your spirit, and let no one deal treacherously against the wife of your youth. For I hate divorce,' says the Lord." Why is cleaving so important to God?

5. What are some reasons commitment is important to a marriage relationship? Why is your mate's commitment important to you?

Make a date with your mate to meet in the next few days to complete **HomeBuilders Project #7.** Your leader will ask at the next session for you to share one thing from this experience.

_____   _____   _____

Date   Time   Location

The Questions Book for Marriage Intimacy by Dennis and Barbara Rainey.

This short book offers 31 questions you've probably never thought to ask your mate. These questions will ignite your curiosity and rekindle your fascination for each other. These questions will spark many memorable hours of sharing, sharpen your understanding of your mate and stimulate closeness in new areas of your marriage.

As a Couple: 5-10 Minutes

Review the first two phases of constructing a great marriage: leave and cleave. Share your responses to the evaluation exercise done during class. Then select one of the following projects that is most relevant to your marriage today.

Individually: 15-20 Minutes

1. Use the following chart to rank yourself and your mate in each area of leaving your parents:

No Dependence on Parents					Total Dependence on Parents
(<———————————————————————————>)					
0	1	2	3	4	5

Yourself		Your Mate
0 1 2 3 4 5	Financial Dependence	0 1 2 3 4 5
0 1 2 3 4 5	Social Dependence	0 1 2 3 4 5
0 1 2 3 4 5	Emotional Dependence	0 1 2 3 4 5
0 1 2 3 4 5	Acceptance & Approval	0 1 2 3 4 5
0 1 2 3 4 5	Loyalty	0 1 2 3 4 5

2. List any actions you may need to take to be more independent of parents or other relatives.

    _____

3. List any suggestions you have for your mate and note how you can help him/her reduce dependence on parents or other relatives.

    _____

    Now turn to the end of the **HomeBuilders Project** and complete the section entitled "Interact as a Couple."

4. Answer the following Yes/No, True/False questions about cleaving to your mate:

Y	N	Do you ever threaten to leave your mate?
T	F	My mate is secure in my commitment to him/her.
T	F	I am more committed to my mate than to my career.
T	F	My mate knows I am more committed to him/her than to my career.
T	F	I am more committed to my mate than to my activities.
Y	N	Do you emotionally leave your mate by withdrawing for an extended period of time because of conflict?

Y   N   Do you mentally leave your mate by staying preoccupied with other things?

Y   N   Are you passive about helping your mate solve his/her problems?

Y   N   Are you interested in your mate's needs and actively doing what you can to meet them?

5. Now go back through the above list and determine in what areas you need to demonstrate a stronger commitment to your mate.

Area	COMMITMENT TO CLEAVE	Action Point

6. Do you need to ask your mate's forgiveness in an area? If so, in which one(s)?

7. Write out your plan for communicating your commitment to your mate. Be specific.

Interact as a Couple: 10 Minutes

1. Share what both of you wrote in completing your project. Look each other in the eyes as you discuss your writings.

2. Work together to identify one or two actions for you to take in the coming week in response to your discussion.

Remember to bring your calendar for **Make a Date** to the next class session.

SESSION 8

Constructing a Relationship: Becoming One Flesh

OBJECTIVES

You will help your group members construct a distinctively Christian marriage as you guide them to:

- Identify the connection between becoming one flesh and achieving oneness, and
- Identify the need to demonstrate transparency with their mates.

COMMENTS

This session deals with the physical aspects of the marriage relationship. At least it deals with the purpose of physical intimacy. Be sensitive that some people in the class may be embarrassed by a discussion on the purpose of sex. Others may see it as an opportunity to revert to adolescent suggestiveness. Your attitude in leading this session will set the tone which others will follow.

The process of becoming one requires that a couple construct their marriage by leaving parents, cleaving to each other and becoming one flesh.

Student is on page 121.

(10-15 Minutes)

*To help each person reflect on key points as well as the **HomeBuilders Project** from Session 7, mount two large sheets of newsprint or poster paper on opposite walls. On one sheet letter: "Phase 1: Leave." On the other one letter: "Phase 2: Cleave." Have ready a supply of markers near each sheet. As people arrive, invite them to write on one sheet an insight they gained from last week's class discussion or from doing the **HomeBuilders Project**. If someone's insight is written by another person, the comment can be underlined, circled or otherwise highlighted to show agreement.*

After most people have had a chance to add a comment or two, invite men and women to form separate small groups of no more than five or six persons per group. Ask each group of men to discuss this question: "When a couple effectively leaves parents and cleaves to each other, what benefits does the husband receive?" Ask the women's groups to answer the same question, identifying benefits to the wife. Allow several minutes for interaction, then invite volunteers to share responses from their group.

Distribute the Session 8 handouts you duplicated.

Comment: *"In Session 7 we saw the first two phases of God's blueprints for the lifelong process of constructing a godly marriage. In this session we will consider the third phase, Becoming One Flesh. The physical aspects of marriage are usually considered in terms of techniques and sensations, with little attention given to the primary God-given purpose of sexual relations. When that purpose is neglected, a couple's sex life becomes a problem rather than a pleasure, and all other aspects of the relationship suffer as well."*

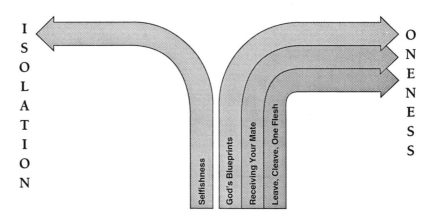

(35-45 Minutes)

Tip: Guide the class as a whole through the following study. Ask for volunteers to read aloud the Scripture verses indicated, then invite others to respond to the questions.

A. Phase 3—Become One Flesh (Genesis 2:24)
(10-15 Minutes)

1. Read Genesis 2:24. The third step in the construction process is to "become one flesh"—to establish physical intimacy. What insights does Matthew 19:6 add to your understanding of becoming one flesh?

    _____

    Answer: The obvious meaning of becoming "one flesh" is for the husband and wife to establish physical intimacy with one another. The Hebrew term "flesh" clearly refers to the body, and the word "one" is from a root meaning "to unify." Matthew 19:6 makes it clear that God not only approves of sexual intimacy in marriage, but is the initiator of the process. No human influences should be allowed to interfere with such a union.

    NOTE: You might find your group becomes a little quiet with these questions about sex. That's okay—it's to be expected.

2. Is becoming one flesh something that happens at a point in time or an ongoing process? Or is it both?

    _____

    Answer: In one sense, physical intimacy is established each time a couple becomes one sexually. In another sense, the intimacy that is gained through sexual union carries over into all other areas of the relationship.

3. Why is becoming one flesh important in achieving oneness in marriage?

    _____

Student is on page 122.

Answer: Physical union is an expression of oneness with the total person, uniting spirit, soul and body.

4. List three of the most romantic times you and your mate have experienced:

_____

Tip: Mention an incident from your marriage before you have each individual respond to this question privately for two or three minutes. Then invite participants to share from their lists.

Look for a common thread in these incidents which drew you together and which you can share with the group.

_____

Tip: After a minute or two in which people think and write, invite volunteers to share the "common thread" they noticed among the incidents they recalled. Some people may identify external factors such as location, timing, preliminary activities, etc. If so, ask "What was it that helped draw you together?"

HOMEBUILDERS PRINCIPLE #7:
A godly marriage is established and experienced as we leave, cleave and become one flesh.

Student is on page 122.

B. The Result—Naked and Unashamed
(10 Minutes)
Give people two or three minutes to think about and write their responses to these first two questions. Then invite volunteers to share their answers.

1. Read Genesis 2:25. The result of Adam and Eve fulfilling the three phases of construction was that they were "naked and unashamed." What is the significance of a couple being "naked and unashamed?" How is this a picture of oneness?

_____

Answer: This meant more than their physical nakedness. It also meant they were completely "transparent" with one another, feeling no threat in revealing themselves to their mate. What better picture of oneness could there be?

2. Physical intimacy obviously contributes to achieving openness and transparency in a marriage. But sexual relations by themselves are no guarantee that such transparency will result. What makes the difference?

Answer: The act of giving and receiving physical pleasure cannot by itself build one-ness. Only when marital sex is within the context of caring and commitment does physical intimacy build lasting emotional intimacy.

3. Why is your acceptance of and commitment to your mate important in achieving openness and transparency in your relationship? What additional light does 1 John 4:18 shed on this process?

Tip: Point out that this question calls for a summary of all that has been discussed in this session, pushing each person to think personally about his or her marriage relationship. After a few moments for thought, invite volunteers to share their responses to the question.

_____

Answer: No one can be fully open with another as long as there is fear of how that person will react. Fear cannot be argued or wished away; only love, expressed in total acceptance and commitment, is strong enough to defeat it.

Student is on page 123.

Make a date with your mate to meet in the next few days to complete *HomeBuilders Project #8*. Your leader will ask at the next session for you to share one thing from this experience.

_____   _____   _____

Date   Time   Location

Staying Close by Dennis Rainey.

Chapters 18-22 contain useful information that expands upon what we've covered in the two sessions on constructing a marriage.

Distribute the HomeBuilders Project #8 handouts. Suggest that couples could share their answers to the evaluation questions at any time after class, or wait until their scheduled HomeBuilders Project time.

> **Comment:** *"The next session, 'Fitting Together,' will focus on God's blueprint of specific responsibilities husbands and wives have in building oneness in their marriages. In order to deal in depth with each partner's role (and to allow each partner the freedom to respond without the mate doing any elbow-jabbing), the entire session will be conducted in separate rooms for men and women. Also, this session will require 30 minutes more time than any of the others."*

Decide on the best starting and ending times to enable group members to make child-care arrangements.

Dismiss with a time of prayer, followed by refreshments and fellowship. Remember to be fair with your group by ending on time, even if some of the content cannot be fully covered.

SESSION 8

Constructing a Relationship: Becoming One Flesh

The process of becoming one requires that a couple construct their marriage by leaving parents, cleaving to each other and becoming one flesh.

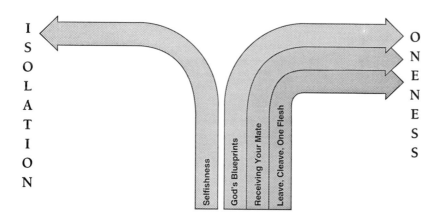

A. Phase 3—Become One Flesh (Genesis 2:24)

1. Read Genesis 2:24. The third step in the construction process is to "become one flesh"—to establish physical intimacy. What insights does Matthew 19:6 add to your understanding of becoming one flesh?

   _____

2. Is becoming one flesh something that happens at a point in time, or an ongoing process? Or is it both?

   _____

3. Why is becoming one flesh important in achieving oneness in marriage?

   _____

4. List three of the most romantic times you and your mate have experienced:

   Look for a common thread in these incidents which drew you together and which you can share with the group.

   _____

HOMEBUILDERS PRINCIPLE #7:

A godly marriage is established and experienced as we leave, cleave and become one flesh.

B. The Result—Naked and Unashamed

1. Read Genesis 2:24. The result of Adam and Eve fulfilling the three phases of construction was that they were "naked and unashamed." What is the significance of a couple's being "naked and unashamed"? How is this a picture of oneness?

   _____

2. Physical intimacy obviously contributes to achieving openness and transparency in a marriage, but sexual relations by themselves are no guarantee that such transparency will result. What makes the difference?

   _____

3. Why is your acceptance of and commitment to your mate important in achieving openness and transparency in your relationship? What additional light does 1 John 4:18 shed on this process?

   _____

Make a date with your mate to meet in the next few days to complete **HomeBuilders Project #8**. Your leader will ask at the next session for you to share one thing from this experience.

| _____ | _____ | _____ |
| Date | Time | Location |

Staying Close by Dennis Rainey.

 Chapters 18-22 contain useful information that expands upon what we've covered in the two sessions on constructing a marriage.

HomeBuilders Project #8

As a Couple: 5-10 Minutes

Review the third phase of constructing a great marriage—becoming one flesh. If you have not already done so, compare answers to the evaluation questions.

Individually: 10-15 Minutes

Becoming One Flesh at a Point in Time

1. How has leaving and cleaving made becoming one flesh easier? What changes do you need to make in these areas?

   _____

2. What circumstances or settings seem best for you to share intimately with one another? List a few.

   _____

3. What attitudes need to be present in you and your mate as you come together?

   _____

4. Write your mate a note: "You please me most when you..."

   _____

Becoming One Flesh over a Lifetime

1. How are you more one flesh now than when you first married?

   _____

2. In what one or two areas of your marriage do you need to continue to work at being one with each other?

   _____

   Now complete the section below.

Interact as a Couple: 10-15 Minutes

1. Share what both of you wrote in completing your project. Look each other in the eyes as you discuss your answers.
2. Work together to identify one or two actions for you to take in the coming week in response to your discussion.
3. Make a date as soon as possible to have a two- or three-hour block of time to be alone together for more communication.

Remember to bring your calendar for **Make a Date** to the next class session.

SESSION 9

HUSBANDS

Fitting Together Part One

OBJECTIVES

You will help the husbands learn to fit together with their wives as you guide them to:

- Identify the biblical responsibilities a husband has to his wife;
- Discuss hurdles that interfere with fulfilling these responsibilities;
- Choose specific actions to fulfill these responsibilities; and
- Commit to being accountable to the other husbands in fulfilling these responsibilities.

COMMENTS

1. In this session and the next, you will split the group into two sections—husbands and wives. Both group leaders should read these two pages.
2. These two sessions tackle one of the most difficult and controversial topics today in the Christian church—roles for husbands and wives. Most couples do not clearly understand what the Bible says about submission and headship, and will come in with preconceived ideas.

    The irony is that no matter how much people believe that there should be no roles in marriage, in reality there are no role-less relationships. Every married couple lives out roles in their relationship to one another, to their children and to others whom they contact.

    It is important that you look through both the men's and women's sections to see what each group will be discussing. More than anything else, you'll need to challenge them to set aside their preconceived ideas and look at what the Bible says about these subjects—not at what they think, or what the culture thinks.

    Also, realize that many of the arguments against defining men's and women's roles have their root in the way men and women have acted out those roles in the past. In the name of "being head of the home," for example, many men have ruled their homes almost as dictators. A true understanding of Scripture should open some eyes.

3. Each group member is asked to become accountable to the group to report back next session on experiences in carrying out the actions planned during this session. Be sensitive to people who may be reluctant to be accountable to the group. Inform all participants, before they select actions to carry out, that they will be asked to be accountable to the group for at least one action they want to do. This sharing is a helpful means of gaining sympathetic support from others who are also working on improving their roles in marriage.

4. You'll need to arrange for a competent leader for the other group. Your mate is probably the logical one to fill this role, but if he or she is uncomfortable with leading, you may prefer to ask another group member to lead.

5. Finally, note that there are more **Construction** exercises than normal—three for the husbands and four for the wives.

There are three biblical responsibilities God wants a husband to assume toward his wife: servant-leader-ship, unselfish loving, and caring.

Student is on page 133.

(15-20 Minutes)

This Warm Up is intended to help the husbands recognize a few challenges involved in being a husband and to admit—at least to themselves—that they need some help in meeting those challenges.

Comment: Begin this session by asking the men in your group to be willing to open up and be honest with this group of men. "There are very few times in life when men really have the opportunity to admit where they need help as husbands. I really want this session to be more than just shallow talking, but as is appropriate, a sharing of what is really going on in your heart, life and role as a husband. That's how we can really come alongside and help one another."

Have two men both share one insight into marriage which they gained from completing HomeBuilders Project #8. Ask for a show of hands from those who did the project. Do not chide those who did not, but encourage them to complete it and if needed, make up unfinished projects. Congratulate those who did and underscore the importance of doing the project for each session.

Lead the group in responding to the following questions:

1. **What various roles must you fill to be a success as a man in our society today?**

_____

Answer: Husband, father, provider, lover, employer/employee, etc. Success today is usually evaluated not in terms of our relationships, but of our status at work, size of our house and our accumulation of wealth.

Tip: As roles are suggested, list them on the chalkboard or an overhead transparency. Then refer to the list as you ask the next question.

2. **What kinds of preparation (schooling, training courses, books, etc.) did you have for filling these roles?**

_____

Answer: Lead the group to see that some roles involve significant training requirements and opportunities, but being a husband is something people seem to expect can be done with little or no preparation. Many men didn't have an effective role model of a husband in their fathers.

Comment: Oneness results when a couple follows God's blueprints, receives one another as God's gift, and then constructs their marriage by leaving parents, cleaving to each other and becoming one flesh. In this session, we will discover what character traits are essential if we are to be the husbands God created us to be.

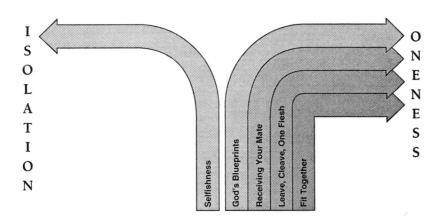

It is vital that you understand from Scripture your responsibility as a husband. Only as you and your wife understand the unique roles which God has given to you can the oneness God intended in marriage be obtained.

Comment: Introduce the topic for this session: "In our culture, there are many voices telling men and women what they ought to be like. Because of the vast changes in women's roles that have occurred during the past two decades, many men find it hard to relate to this 'new woman.' It will not be possible in this session to answer all the needs and questions which may be raised. Even though you may feel somewhat frustrated that some issue did not get explored as thoroughly as you wished, our goal is that you will come out of this with at least one or two actions to help you more successfully fit yourself with your wife in your role as husband."

(60-70 Minutes)

Because there is a great deal of confusion about the roles of men and women today, this session will be spent helping you write a biblical job description for being a husband—the head of your home.

As you begin this segment, read aloud the following paragraph: "The remainder of this session deals with 'core roles,' not comprehensive lifestyles or specific tasks. These roles are never presented as describing the totality of a person's life, but as a central focus around which a person may build varied interests and involvements. All other forms of employment, recreation and ministry will naturally vary in intensity and importance in different stages of life. At no time, however, can husband or wife allow any other enterprise to infringe upon or usurp his or her core role. It is crucial to avoid the common errors of either throwing out the biblical roles or forcing people to limit themselves totally within those roles. While people may have many questions and misgivings at this point, assure them that God's intent for their marriage is always for their benefit. The core roles are best because they are part of God's perfect design."

By stressing both mutual responsibility to the core roles and flexibility and creativity in building a lifestyle around them, you will help participants get over the emotional threat and misunderstanding that some will bring to this topic.

Distribute copies of the Session 9 (Husbands) handouts you duplicated.

The First Responsibility—Becoming A Servant Leader
(20-25 Minutes)

Student is on page 134.

Comment: "The responsibility of husbands which is most frequently mentioned in the Bible is that of leadership in the home. However, there are many different ideas of what leadership involves. Many men have justified very selfish actions which are in complete opposition to the biblical goal of oneness, claiming the Bible supports their demands for privileges as 'head of the house.'"

Option: Ask group members to identify some typical images of leadership which are common in our society (the drill sergeant, the football coach, the corporation executive, the orchestra conductor, dictator, etc.). After a variety of leadership roles have been mentioned, ask the men to suggest personal qualities that society associates with these leaders (strength, authority, power, dominance, decisiveness, superiority, knowledge, a person who never admits having needs, etc.). Point out that in order to build oneness in a marriage, a husband needs to be careful to take his model of leadership from Scripture, not from society.

1. How is a husband's position as leader illustrated in Ephesians 5:23?

   _____

   Answer: Husband leads the wife as Christ leads the church.

   Tip: Point out that leadership is much more of a responsibility than a privilege.

2. What are the responsibilities involved in being "the head" of your wife, a group of people or an organization?

   _____

   Answer: Accept the answers that are suggested, making sure that various facets of responsibility are mentioned: being aware of all factors in a situation, being sensitive to the needs and desires of those involved, helping those involved to succeed, making decisions, and accepting the consequences of the decisions.

3. What additional insights do you gain about leadership from Mark 10:42-45? What is servant-leadership?

   _____

   Answer: Jesus made a clear contrast between the "superior leader," who focuses on authority and status, and the "servant-leader," who focuses on giving of self to the ones he leads. The servant-leader does not lord authority over others, but willingly serves the needs of all. He does not demand service from others; rather, he gives up his own life and desires for others to have life—whether they deserve it or not.

4. **Which of those concepts is the most challenging to you as you think of your leadership in your home? Why?**

_____

Tip: Instruct each man to write down a brief response to this question. After two or three minutes, read your answer, then ask volunteers to read what they wrote down. After several have responded, invite answers to Question 5.

5. **How would becoming a servant-leader change a man who:**
   a. **tends to be *passive* and not accept his responsibilities?**

_____

Answer: This wouldn't mean attempting to transform his personality to become a "take charge" type of man, because God doesn't want him to become something he isn't. It would mean taking his responsibilities seriously and begin initiating opportunities to serve his wife and meet her needs. Also, many husbands like this tend to let their wives do much of the work around the house—cleaning, caring for children, etc. It would mean getting involved.

   b. **is *dictatorial* and refuses to listen to his wife?**

_____

Answer: A dictatorial leader is the opposite of a servant-leader. A husband like this would need to begin looking for ways to serve instead of control. He would involve his wife in decisions, and would be concerned with her fulfillment. When there's a disagreement, it might even mean making a conscious choice to put aside his own desires and go by what his wife wants. It also would mean taking a strong look at how he can get involved with his wife in household responsibilities and child-rearing.

6. **How would becoming a servant-leader affect the ability of your wife to submit (fit herself) to your leadership?**

_____

Answer: Many husbands complain about their wives, but fail to look at how they are doing in their own role as servant-leader.

A husband's servant-leadership is the only thing that makes a wife's submission reasonable. A passive husband makes submission impossible and a domineering husband makes submission intolerable. True submission is a response to a husband's true servant-leadership.

Tip: Point out that one of the roles the wives are examining is that of submission. Here is some of what they're learning:

- *The biblical view of submission is very different from the common ideas of inferiority, loss of identity, or blind obedience that many people assume.*
- *Submission comes from two Greek words meaning "under" and "arrange or complete." The sense of the term is to voluntarily organize or fit into or under in a way that makes a complete whole.*
- *Submission does not require a wife to violate other scriptural commands or principles. The Bible does not ask wives to submit to sinful or damaging demands.*

7. List one to three practical ways in which you can demonstrate servant-leadership to your wife in the coming weeks:

   _____

Tip: After allowing time for men to write their ideas for number 7, invite volunteers to share one idea from their list. Suggest that any ideas that are shared are fair game for others to add to their own lists if they so desire.

Comment: "Later in the session each man will be asked to choose one specific action and to be accountable to the group to carry it out before the next session."

Option: If time allows (and the wives' session is still going strong) lead the men in planning a surprise for the wives at the conclusion of this study. Consider a dinner out, a concert, play, picnic, party, etc.

HOMEBUILDERS PRINCIPLE FOR MEN #1:

A husband who is becoming a servant-leader is one who is in the process of denying himself daily for his wife.

Student is on page 135.

Make a date with your mate to meet in the next few days to complete *HomeBuilders Project #9*.

Date	Time	Location

Rejoin the wives for a few moments to have the couples make a date to complete HomeBuilders Project #9 this week. Distribute the HomeBuilders Project pages you duplicated.

Rocking the Roles by Robert Lewis and William Hendricks.

This book provides a balanced, biblical guide to understanding marital roles.

Building Your Mate's Self-Esteem by Dennis and Barbara Rainey.

In this book you will find clues to understanding your wife's self-esteem, laws that will help you to free your mate from her past and building blocks to strengthen her self-esteem.

The Questions Book for Marriage Intimacy by Dennis and Barbara Rainey.

This short book offers 31 questions you've probably never thought to ask your mate. These questions will ignite your curiosity and rekindle your fascination for each other. These questions will spark many memorable hours of sharing, sharpen your understanding of your mate and stimulate closeness in new areas of your marriage.

Staying Close by Dennis Rainey.

Chapter 14—"The Making of a Servant-leader"—elaborates on the material covered in this session.

Conclude the session with prayer. Because of the extended time schedule for this session, it may be too late for people to remain for refreshments and fellowship. Be considerate of people's schedules in making your decision.

SESSION 9

Fitting Together Part One

There are three biblical responsibilities God wants a husband to assume toward his wife: servant-leadership, unselfish loving, and caring.

It is vital that you understand from Scripture your responsibility as a husband. Only as you and your wife understand the unique roles which God has given to you can the oneness God intended in marriage be obtained.

1. What various roles must you fill to be a success as a man in our society today?

    _____

2. What kinds of preparation (schooling, training courses, books, etc.) did you have for filling these roles?

    _____

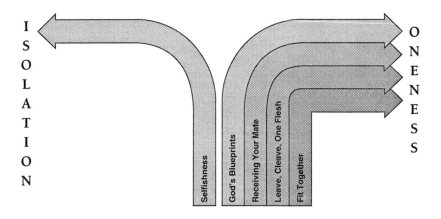

Because there is a great deal of confusion about the roles of men and women today, this session will be spent helping you write a biblical job description for being a husband—the head of your home.

The First Responsibility—Becoming a Servant Leader

1. How is a husband's position as leader illustrated in Ephesians 5:23?

2. What are the responsibilities involved in being "the head" of your wife, a group of people or an organization?

3. What additional insights do you gain about leadership from Mark 10:42-45? What is servant-leadership?

4. Which of those concepts is the most challenging to you as you think of your leadership in your home? Why?

5. How would becoming a servant-leader change a man who:
   a. tends to be **passive** and not accept his responsibilities?

   b. is **dictatorial** and refuses to listen to his wife?

6. How would becoming a servant-leader affect the ability of your wife to submit (fit herself) to your leadership?

7. List one to three practical ways in which you can demonstrate servant-leadership to your wife in the coming weeks:

_____

HOMEBUILDERS PRINCIPLE FOR MEN #1:

A husband who is becoming a servant-leader is one who is in the process of denying himself daily for his wife.

Make a date with your mate to meet in the next few days to complete **HomeBuilders Project #9**.

| _____ | _____ | _____ |
| Date | Time | Location |

Rocking the Roles by Robert Lewis and William Hendricks.

This book provides a balanced, biblical guide to understanding marital roles.

Building Your Mate's Self-Esteem by Dennis and Barbara Rainey.

In this book you will find clues to understanding your wife's self-esteem, laws that will help you to free your mate from her past and building blocks to strengthen her self-esteem.

The Questions Book for Marriage Intimacy by Dennis and Barbara Rainey.

This short book offers 31 questions you've probably never thought to ask your mate. These questions will ignite your curiosity and rekindle your fascination for each other. These questions will spark many memorable hours of sharing, sharpen your understanding of your mate and stimulate closeness in new areas of your marriage.

Staying Close by Dennis Rainey.

Chapter 14—"The Making of a Servant-leader"—elaborates on the material covered in this session.

As a Couple: 5-10 Minutes

Review what you learned from your class time regarding your respective roles in your marriage.

Individually: 15-20 Minutes

1. What role on this spectrum do you enact in your marriage?

   _____

   Passivist   Servant   Servant-Leader   Leader   Dictator

   What do you need to do to move closer to God's ideal for your role?

   _____

2. List the ways in which you demonstrate servant-leadership in your marriage.

   _____

3. List some areas where you need to improve as a servant-leader.

   _____

   Choose at least one of these areas to work on in the coming weeks. How will you put this into action this week?

   _____

4. Prayerfully ask God to show you how to be a better servant-leader in your home.

Interact as a Couple: 5-10 Minutes

1. Share with one another one way in which you feel your mate is fulfilling his or her role.
2. Have you had your two- to three-hour block of time to be alone together for more communication as mentioned in **HomeBuilders Project #8**? If not make that commitment right now.

Remember to bring your calendar for **Make a Date** to the next class session.

SESSION 9

WIVES

Fitting Together Part One

OBJECTIVES

You will help the wives learn to fit together with their husbands as you guide them to:

- Identify four biblical responsibilities a wife has to her husband;
- Discuss hurdles that interfere with fulfilling these responsibilities;
- Choose specific actions to fulfill these responsibilities; and
- Commit to being accountable to the other wives in fulfilling these responsibilities.

COMMENTS

1. In this session and the next, you will split the class into two sections—husbands and wives. Both group leaders should read these two pages.

2. These two sessions tackle one of the most difficult and controversial topics today in the Christian church—roles for husbands and wives. Most couples do not clearly understand what the Bible says about submission and headship, and will come in with preconceived ideas.

   The irony is that no matter how much people believe that there should be no roles in marriage, in reality there are no role-less relationships. Every married couple lives out roles in their relationship to one another, to their children and to others whom they contact.

   It is important that you look through both the men's and women's sections to see what each group will be discussing. More than anything else, you'll need to challenge them to set aside their preconceived ideas and look at what the Bible says about these subjects—not at what they think or what the culture thinks.

   Also, realize that many of the arguments against defining men's and women's roles have their root in the way men and women have acted out those roles in the past. In the name of "being head of the home," for example, many men have ruled their homes almost as dictators. A true understanding of Scripture should open some eyes.

3. Each group member is asked to become accountable to the group to report back next session on experiences in carrying out the actions planned during this session. Be sensitive to people who may be reluctant to be accountable to the group. Inform all participants, before they select actions to carry out, that they will be asked to be accountable to the group for at least one action they want to do. This sharing is a helpful means of gaining sympathetic support from others who are also working on improving their roles in marriage.

4. You'll need to arrange for a competent leader for the other group. Your mate is probably the logical one to fill this role, but if he or she is uncomfortable with leading, you may prefer to ask another class member to lead.

5. Be aware that as these women come together, each one has different needs. One may just need to talk about the pressures she faces and listen to others do the same. Another woman may be angry and bitter about what the Bible says and find herself rebelling against what Scripture says she should do. Another may be discouraged because her husband gives no leadership and has the wrong priorities, making it extremely difficult for her to be supportive. And others will be very teachable, eager to learn and grow.

   If a woman expresses anger or bitterness, it is best to thank her for being open with the group, then ask her to hold off making any final judgments until she has had an opportunity to consider the complete teaching of this session. Unless she raises issues which others in the group indicate are significant for them as well, it is better to meet with her privately after the session than to take more of the group's time to deal with her individual concerns.

There are four biblical responsibilities God wants a wife to assume toward her husband: making marriage a priority, unselfish love, submission, and respect.

Student is on
page 147.

(10-15 Minutes)

*This **Warm Up** is intended to help the wives recognize a few challenges involved in being a wife and admit—at least to themselves, if not to the group—that they need some help in meeting those challenges.*

> ***Comment:** Begin this session by asking two women who completed HomeBuilders Project #8 to share one insight into marriage which was gained from completing that project. (The purpose of this is accountability.) Congratulate those who did the project and underscore the importance of doing the project for each session.*

> *Distribute the Session 9 (Wives) handouts you duplicated.*

1. List some words that describe each point of view:

	Society's View	God's View
Woman		
Wife		
Mother		

Tip: Lead the group in working together to complete this chart. The second column of the chart will probably be harder to complete, illustrating the need to examine what Scripture indicates is God's view of a wife.

2. Women are being told today that they need to be successful. What do you think makes a successful wife?

Tip: After several people have commented, follow up with this question: "What impact do you think the changing roles of men and women have had on wives, husbands and marriage?" Allow several minutes for discussion.

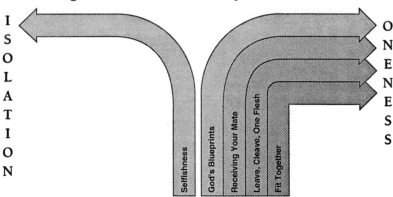

It is vital that you understand from Scripture your responsibility as a wife. Only as you and your husband understand the unique roles which God has given to you can the oneness God intended in marriage be obtained.

Comment: Summarize your opening discussion and introduce the topic for this session: "In our culture, there are many voices telling men and women what they ought to be like. Because of the vast changes in women's roles that have occurred during the past few decades, many women find it difficult to relate to their role as a 'new woman.' It will not be possible in this one session to answer all the needs and questions that may be raised. So, even though it is likely you may feel frustrated that some issue was not explored as thoroughly as you wished, our goal is that you will come out of this with at least one or two actions to help you more deeply value your home and to help you successfully fit yourself with your husband."

(65-75 Minutes)

Tip: As you begin this segment, read aloud the following paragraph: "The remainder of this session deals with 'core roles,' not comprehensive lifestyles or specific tasks. These roles are never presented as describing the totality of a person's life, but as a central focus around which a person may build varied interests and involvements. All other forms of employment, recreation and ministry will naturally vary in intensity and importance in different stages of life. At no time, however, can husband or wife allow any other enterprise to infringe upon or usurp his or her core role. It is crucial to avoid the common errors of either throwing out the biblical roles or forcing people to limit themselves totally within those roles. While people may have many questions and misgivings at this point, assure them that God's intent for their marriages is always for their benefit. The core roles are best because they are part of God's perfect design."

By stressing both mutual responsibility to the core roles and flexibility and creativity in building a lifestyle around them, you will help participants get over the emotional threat and misunderstanding that some will bring to this topic.

A. The First Responsibility—Making Your Marriage a Priority
(20-25 Minutes)

Student is on page 148.

Tip: Explain that the last 21 verses of Proverbs describe "an excellent wife."

1. What does it mean for a wife to look "well to the ways of her household" (Proverbs 31:27)?

    _____

    Answer: "Look well" conveys the idea that a wife is alert to the needs of her home. That, in turn, means that she makes it a priority.

2. What happens to your relationship with your husband when you do or do not "look well" to your marriage?

WHEN I DO "LOOK WELL"	WHEN I DO NOT "LOOK WELL"

3. In the "IDEAL WIFE" column below, rank these items by numbering them from 1-13 to show the priorities that make a successful wife. Then, in the "ME" column, show where your priorities currently are.

IDEAL WIFE	ME		IDEAL WIFE	ME		IDEAL WIFE	ME	
☐	☐	Children	☐	☐	House/Yard	☐	☐	Husband
☐	☐	Education	☐	☐	Job/Career	☐	☐	Friends
☐	☐	Relatives	☐	☐	Community Service	☐	☐	Church
☐	☐	Social Activities	☐	☐	Appearance	☐	☐	TV
			☐	☐	Relationship with God			

Tip: Expect some differences in the relative ranking of the various items, but point out that the major tenet of this study is that "Relationship with God" and "Husband" need to be #1 and #2 in order for a wife to be building a marriage according to God's blueprints. Point out that very good and even necessary things, (church, kids, community service, etc.) can drain what she has to offer her marriage.

Ask each person to go through the list of items again, this time marking in the "ME" column the order of importance she actually gave each item during the last week. After two or three minutes, divide the group into pairs. If there is an uneven number in the group, work as a partner with one person. Instruct each woman to share with her partner two items which most closely matched her ranking for the "Ideal Wife" and two items which were furthest out of line with the ideal. Allow several minutes for discussion.

Invite volunteers to tell what discussing this chart has said to them about where their main priorities should be and how they feel they are doing in that area.

4. How is the priority you place on your marriage reflected in your schedule?

   _____

   Tip: Call on one or two women to share how making marriage more of a priority would be reflected in her schedule. Be prepared to share any insights from your experience in scheduling your time to develop your relationship with your husband.

5. What are the biggest obstacles you face in making your marriage a priority?

   _____

6. What are three things that you can do to make your relationship with your husband your priority in the coming week? Be specific, practical and make it personal.

   _____

   Tip: After several minutes, divide the group into pairs and have each woman share one answer she wrote, telling why she feels it is significant in her relationship with her husband.

HOMEBUILDERS PRINCIPLE FOR WOMEN #1:

Becoming a successful wife requires that a woman make her husband her #2 priority after her relationship with God.

Tip: Call attention to HomeBuilders Principle for Women #1 as a summary of this discussion.

B. The Second Responsibility—Unselfish Love
(10 minutes)

Student is on page 149.

1. A problem in our society is that "love" is usually equated with a feeling. We need to look at Scripture to find the full definition of what love is. Write down the characteristics of love identified in the following Scriptures:

   Tip: Assign each pair of women one of these passages which describe love. (If you have fewer than six women in the group, assign each person one passage to read and consider.) After two or three minutes, ask each pair (or individual) to share what they discovered.
   1 Corinthians 13:4-7

   _____

   Answer: Patient, kind, not jealous, not bragging, not arrogant, not selfish, etc.
   John 15:13

   _____

   Answer: Giving up her own life and desires for the one loved.
   Philippians 2:3,4

   _____

   Answer: Humble, regarding the one loved as being more important than self.

2. Which of these descriptions of love is the most challenging to you in thinking about your relationship with your husband? Why?

   _____

   Tip: Share your own response in this time of personal expression.

3. "The heart of her husband trusts in her" (Proverbs 31:11). Every wife wants a husband who is open, who will share his innermost person with her. Few women, however, realize how insecure and fearful their husbands sometimes are. Your love for your husband has a profound impact on his trust of you and his willingness to be vulnerable (transparent) to you. Remember, biblical love always means seeking the highest good for the person loved; it focuses on actions, not emotions. A wife who commits to doing what is the highest good for her husband will earn her husband's trust.

   Evaluate your husband's openness and trust toward you. How is your love affecting his willingness and ability to be transparent with you?

   _____

4. In order to unselfishly love your husband and open your relationship, what rights are you clinging to and need to let go of?

   _____

5. What three things communicate love to your husband? (Not what you think communicates love, but what he thinks.)

_____

6. What practical way can you demonstrate unselfish love to your husband this week?

_____

Tip: After several minutes, ask each woman to tell one answer she wrote. Share an answer of your own as part of this time of personal expression.

HOMEBUILDERS PRINCIPLE FOR WOMEN #2:

The wife who is becoming an unselfish lover of her husband is one who is putting her husband's needs above her own.

Student is on page 150.

Make a date with your mate to meet in the next few days to complete *HomeBuilders Project #9*. Your leader will ask at the next session for you to share one thing from this experience.

Date	Time	Location

Rejoin the husbands for a few moments to have the couples make a date to complete HomeBuilders Project #9 this week.

Distribute the HomeBuilders Project pages you duplicated. Point out that this week's project requires between 60 and 90 minutes. There are separate projects for husbands and wives, both of which focus on identifying and meeting each other's needs. Couples should do their projects at the same time so that they can check with each other to see if they have accurately listed each other's needs.

Recommended Reading

Rocking the Roles by Robert Lewis and William Hendricks.

This book provides a balanced, biblical guide to understanding marital roles.

Building Your Mate's Self-Esteem by Dennis and Barbara Rainey.

In this book you will find clues to understanding your husband's self-esteem, laws that will help you to free your mate from his past and building blocks to strengthen his self-esteem.

The Questions Book for Marriage Intimacy by Dennis and Barbara Rainey.

This short book offers 31 questions you've probably never thought to ask your mate. These questions will ignite your curiosity and rekindle your fascination for each other. These questions will spark many memorable hours of sharing, sharpen your understanding of your mate and stimulate closeness in new areas of your marriage.

Staying Close by Dennis Rainey.

Chapter 15—"How to Love Your Husband" expands on the material discussed in this session.

Conclude the session with prayer. Because of the extended time schedule for this session, it may be too late for people to remain for refreshments and fellowship. Be considerate of people's schedules in making your decision.

SESSION 9

Fitting Together Part One

There are four biblical responsibilities God wants a wife to assume toward her husband: making marriage a priority, unselfish love, submission, and respect.

1. List some words that describe each point of view:

	Society's View	God's View
Woman		
Wife		
Mother		

2. Women are being told today that they need to be successful. What do you think makes a successful wife?

_____

3. What are some of your struggles in trying to succeed as a wife?

_____

Oneness results when a couple follows God's blueprints, receives one another as God's gift, and then constructs their marriage by leaving parents, cleaving to each other and becoming one flesh.

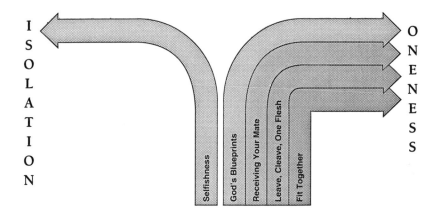

It is vital that you understand from Scripture your responsibility as a wife. Only as you and your husband understand the unique roles which God has given to you can the oneness God intended in marriage be obtained.

A. The First Responsibility—Making Your Marriage a Priority

1. What does it mean for a wife to look "well to the ways of her household" (Proverbs 31:27)?

    _____

2. What happens to your relationship with your husband when you do or do not "look well" to your marriage?

WHEN I DO "LOOK WELL"	WHEN I DO NOT "LOOK WELL"

3. In the "IDEAL WIFE" column below, rank these items by numbering them from

1-13 to show the priorities that make a successful wife. Then, in the "ME" column, show where your priorities currently are.

IDEAL WIFE	ME		IDEAL WIFE	ME		IDEAL WIFE	ME	
☐	☐	Children	☐	☐	House/Yard	☐	☐	Husband
☐	☐	Education	☐	☐	Job/Career	☐	☐	Friends
☐	☐	Relatives	☐	☐	Community Service	☐	☐	Church
☐	☐	Social Activities	☐	☐	Appearance	☐	☐	TV
			☐	☐	Relationship with God			

4. How is the priority you place on your marriage reflected in your schedule?

_____

5. What are the biggest obstacles you face in making your marriage a priority?

_____

6. What are three things that you can do to make your relationship with your husband your priority in the coming week? Be specific, practical and make it personal.

_____

HOMEBUILDERS PRINCIPLE FOR WOMEN #1:

Becoming a successful wife requires that a woman make her husband her #2 priority after her relationship with God.

B. The Second Responsibility—Unselfish Love

1. A problem in our society is that "love" is usually equated with a feeling. We need to look at Scripture to find the full definition of what love is. Write down the characteristics of love identified in the following Scriptures:

   1 Corinthians 13:4-7

   _____

   John 15:13

   _____

   Philippians 2:3,4

   _____

2. Which of these descriptions of love is the most challenging to you in thinking about your relationship with your husband? Why?

   _____

3. "The heart of her husband trusts in her" (Proverbs 31:11). Every wife wants a hus-

band who is open, who will share his innermost person with her. Few women, however, realize how insecure and fearful their husbands sometimes are. Your love for your husband has a profound impact on his trust of you and his willingness to be vulnerable (transparent) to you. Remember, biblical love always means seeking the highest good for the person loved; it focuses on actions and not emotions. A wife who commits to doing what is the highest good for her husband will earn her husband's trust.

Evaluate your husband's openness and trust toward you. How is your love affecting his willingness and ability to be transparent with you?

_____

4.   In order to unselfishly love your husband and open your relationship, what rights are you clinging to and need to let go of?

_____

5.   What three things communicate love to your husband? (Not what **you** think communicates love, but what **he** thinks.)

_____

6.   What practical way can you demonstrate unselfish love to your husband this week?

_____

HOMEBUILDERS PRINCIPLE FOR WOMEN #2:

The wife who is becoming an unselfish lover of her husband is one who is putting her husband's needs above her own.

Make a date with your mate to meet in the next few days to complete **HomeBuilders Project #9**. Your leader will ask at the next session for you to share one thing from this experience.

_____   _____   _____

Date   Time   Location

Recommended Reading

Rocking the Roles by Robert Lewis and William Hendricks.

This book provides a balanced, biblical guide to understanding marital roles.

Building Your Mate's Self-Esteem by Dennis and Barbara Rainey.

In this book you will find clues to understanding your husband's self-esteem, laws that will help you to free your mate from his past and building blocks to strengthen his self-esteem.

The Questions Book for Marriage Intimacy by Dennis and Barbara Rainey.

This short book offers 31 questions you've probably never thought to ask your mate. These questions will ignite your curiosity and rekindle your fascination for each other. These questions will spark many memorable hours of sharing, sharpen your understanding of your mate and stimulate closeness in new areas of your marriage.

Staying Close by Dennis Rainey.

Chapter 15—"How to Love Your Husband" expands on the material discussed in this session.

HomeBuilders Project #9
Wives

As a Couple: 5-10 Minutes

Review what you learned from your class time regarding your respective roles in your marriage.

Individually: 15-20 Minutes

1. How can you demonstrate to your husband this week that he is your second priority (after the Lord)?

   _____

2. Of the three things you listed in the lesson that communicate love to your husband, which one will you implement this week and how?

   _____

3. Prayerfully ask the Lord to reveal to you ways that you have injured your husband's trust in you. Do you need to ask for forgiveness? What can you do to rebuild his trust in this area?

   _____

4. Ask God to show you how to set right priorities and to communicate unselfish love to your husband to build his trust in you.

Interact as a Couple: 5-10 Minutes

1. Share with one another one way in which you feel your mate is fulfilling his or her role.
2. Have you had your two- to three-hour block of time to be alone together for more communication as mentioned in **HomeBuilders Project #8**? If not make that commitment right now.

Remember to bring your calendar for **Make a Date** to the next session.

SESSION 10

HUSBANDS

Fitting Together Part Two

OBJECTIVES

You will help the husbands learn to fit together with their wives as you guide them to:

- Identify the biblical responsibilities a husband has to his wife;
- Discuss hurdles that interfere with fulfilling these responsibilities;
- Choose specific actions to fulfill these responsibilities; and
- Commit to being accountable to the other husbands in fulfilling these responsibilities.

There are three biblical responsibilities God wants a husband to assume toward his wife: servant-leadership, unselfish loving, and caring.

*Student is on
page 161.*

(15-20 Minutes)

What factors in society and within marriage make it difficult today to be an effective husband? What are your greatest struggles in being a good husband?

Possible Answers: In society, we're under pressure to succeed in our careers, and sometimes to spend extra hours at work. After years of attacks in our culture on the roles of men and women, many men are unsure of how to relate to their wives. Our culture is so saturated with sexual images that it can be hard to remain true to your wife.

Within marriage: Usually we're unprepared to deal with differences between men and women, and the different needs and desires both sexes bring into a relationship. Add this to the natural selfishness of human beings, and it's difficult to maintain a good relationship.

Tip: Allow several minutes for discussion of Question 3. If some men begin to vent frustrations about their wives or about women in general, explain that the focus of this session will not be on pointing out where our wives may be off base, but to discover ways men can become more successful as husbands.

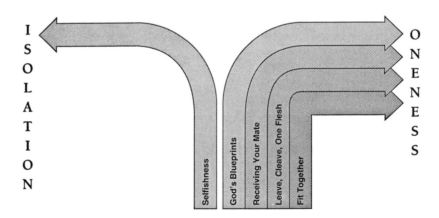

Blueprints

(65-75 Minutes)

A. The Second Responsibility—Unselfish Loving
(20 Minutes)

Student is on page 162.

1. According to Ephesians 5:25-27, why is the second responsibility of a husband so important?

   Answer: Leadership that is not motivated by love can lead to tyranny, and servitude that is not motivated by love will lead to drudgery and resentment. The key to love is that it is unselfish, not trying to possess the beloved, but to benefit her. Unselfish love is always demonstrated by giving of self, not just of things.

   Tip: If the discussion on Question 1 begins to touch on the wife's reaction to unselfish love, call attention to the next question.

2. How does this kind of love, this denial of self, communicate love to your wife? Why is this so important?

   _____

   Answer: Many wives have not seen their husbands deny themselves since courtship, and many others have never seen it at all. A husband's unselfish love frees the wife from her own selfishness, defeating isolation and building oneness.

3. How does God describe love in these other passages?

   Tip: Divide the group into thirds. Assign the men in each group one of the following Scriptures to read and then report (after two or three minutes) on ways God describes love.

   Philippians 2:3

   _____

   Answer: Humble, regarding the one loved as being more important than self.

155

1 Corinthians 13:4-7

Answer: Patient, kind, not jealous, not bragging, not arrogant, not selfish, etc.

John 15:13

Answer: Gives up his own life and desires for the one loved.

4. Which of the preceding descriptions of love is the most meaningful to you? Why?

Tip: Share your own response, then invite volunteers to do likewise.

5. Which of those descriptions of love does your wife need most? How can you demonstrate that love to her?

6. What would you have to do in this self-denial to make it a willing act of love and not a grudging duty?

Tip: Point out (if it has not already been mentioned in the discussion) that any act of self-denial will only communicate love if it is perceived as being done willingly. Ask the men to suggest things they might need to do to ensure that they communicate willingness and not reluctance. (Focus on the value of the person, not on the act itself. A good question to ask is, "Why is she worth it?")

HOMEBUILDERS PRINCIPLE FOR MEN #2:

The husband who is becoming an unselfish lover of his wife is one who is putting his wife's needs above his own.

Student is on page 162.

B. The Third Responsibility—Caring (20-25 Minutes)

1. What does Ephesians 5:28-30 add to your view of your responsibility to your wife? Why is this truth important?

Answer: Loving a wife is compared with concern for a man's own body, indicating the highest level of care growing out of very intimate knowledge. Demonstrating unselfish love and care for a wife is the best means by which a husband's own needs *are met. Caring involves nourishing (fostering growth and maturity) and cherishing (esteeming someone as a priority). Again, the example of Jesus is the standard to imitate for those who belong to Him.*

Option: As each idea is suggested, ask the group to identify a specific example of how that truth could be put into practice within a husband-wife relationship. For example:

- *A man who seeks to love his wife as his own body would seek to understand and then care for his wife's needs.*
- *A man who cares for his wife's needs first will find her capable of meeting his needs in return.*
- *A man can nourish his wife by encouraging her to pursue areas in which she wants to grow (by studying, taking classes, trying new ways of doing things, etc.).*
- *A man can cherish his wife by scheduling time with her as a priority before other demands fill his calendar.*
- A man can learn to follow Christ's example of caring by regularly studying the biblical accounts of Jesus' life and praying for God's help to apply Jesus' example to specific family situations.

Tip: Divide the class into small groups of no more than five men per group. Assign half of the groups to discuss Question 2 while the rest of the groups discuss Question 3. Allow several minutes for interaction, then invite people from each group to report on the ideas they thought of for nourishing and cherishing their wives. Suggest that as the men listen to these reports, they write down ideas that seem to fit their own wives.

2. "Nourish" means to foster growth. What elements of nourishment does your wife need from you to help her grow?

3. The term "cherish" is from the Greek word meaning "to incubate or brood," and indicates esteeming someone as a priority. How can you show your wife you esteem and value her? Be specific.

Comment: "Just as the wife's submission enables the husband to fulfill his role as servant-leader, so the husband's honor and praise enable the wife to fulfill her calling. The core roles can only be adequately fulfilled when the mate responds properly.

"While we often hear exhortations for wives to submit, we rarely hear about the masculine counterpart to submission—honor and praise. Any man who is serious about his wife fulfilling her role will make honor and praise priority ingredients in his response to her efforts. Without these she will feel that her role and tasks are inferior and secondary and will do what so many women in our society have done—go looking for something else that will make her feel good about herself."

4. One aspect of leadership is bringing appropriate resources to a situation to help others become successful. What resources do you need to use in order to nourish and cherish your wife so she can succeed as a woman, wife and mother (help with her schedule, assist with a problem, give or get direct help with a task, provide encouragement, spend time with her, etc.)?

_____

Tip: Instruct each man to write down two or three specific ideas of his own, either personalizing one of those suggested or adding a new one. After several minutes, invite volunteers to share at least one idea they wrote.

HOMEBUILDERS PRINCIPLE FOR MEN #3:

The husband who is becoming a caring head of his house is one who encourages his wife to grow and become all that God intended her to be.

Choose one act of servant-leadership, unselfish loving, or caring for your wife which you will share with one other man in our group and for which you will agree to be accountable to the group by the next session.

_____

Option: You may want to pair the men off (especially if you have already been having couples maintain contact with each other between the sessions) and have them check with each other before the next session to see how each is doing in carrying out his plan. Guide the group in dividing into pairs. If the number of men is unequal, join with one person yourself. Instruct them to pray together concerning their efforts to fulfill their responsibilities as husbands.

Make a Date

Student is on page 163.

Make a date with your mate to meet in the next few days to complete *HomeBuilders Project #10*.

_____   _____   _____
    Date   Time   Location

Rejoin the wives for a few moments to have the couples make a date to complete HomeBuilders Project #10 this week.

Distribute the HomeBuilders Project pages you duplicated. Point out that this week's project requires between sixty and ninety minutes. There are separate projects for husbands and wives, both of which focus on identifying and meeting each other's needs. While the projects are to be done separately, suggest that they do them at the same time so that at an agreed-upon time they can check with each other to see if they have accurately listed each other's needs.

Recommended Reading

Rocking the Roles by Robert Lewis and William Hendricks.

This book provides a balanced, biblical guide to understanding marital roles.

Building Your Mate's Self-Esteem by Dennis and Barbara Rainey.

In this book you will find clues to understanding your wife's self-esteem, laws that will help you to free your mate from her past and building blocks to strengthen her self-esteem.

The Questions Book for Marriage Intimacy by Dennis and Barbara Rainey.

This short book offers 31 questions you've probably never thought to ask your mate. These questions will ignite your curiosity and rekindle your fascination for each other. These questions will spark many memorable hours of sharing, sharpen your understanding of your mate and stimulate closeness in new areas of your marriage.

Staying Close by Dennis Rainey.

Chapter 14—"The Making of a Servant-leader"—elaborates on the material covered in this session.

Conclude the session with prayer. Because of the extended time schedule for this session, it may be too late for people to remain for refreshments and fellowship. Be considerate of people's schedules in making your decision.

SESSION 10

Fitting Together
Part Two

There are three biblical responsibilities God wants a husband to assume toward his wife: servant-leadership, unselfish loving, and caring.

What factors in society and within marriage make it difficult today to be an effective husband? What are your greatest struggles in being a good husband?

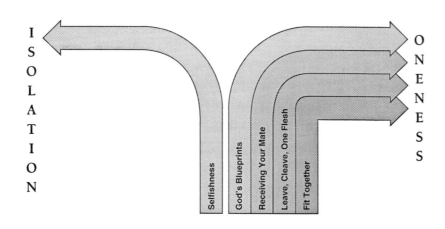

ISOLATION

ONENESS

Selfishness

God's Blueprints

Receiving Your Mate

Leave, Cleave, One Flesh

Fit Together

161

Blueprints

A. The Second Responsibility—Unselfish Loving

1. According to Ephesians 5:25-27, why is the second responsibility of a husband so important?

   _____

2. How does this kind of love, this denial of self, communicate love to your wife? Why is this so important?

   _____

3. How does God describe love in these other passages?
   Philippians 2:3

   _____

   1 Corinthians 13:4-7

   _____

   John 15:13

4. Which of the preceding descriptions of love is the most meaningful to you? Why?

   _____

5. Which of those descriptions of love does your wife need most? How can you demonstrate that love to her?

   _____

6. What would you have to do in this self-denial to make it a willing act of love and not a grudging duty?

   _____

HOMEBUILDERS PRINCIPLE FOR MEN #2:

The husband who is becoming an unselfish lover of his wife is one who is putting his wife's needs above his own.

B. The Third Responsibility—Caring

1. What does Ephesians 5:28-30 add to your view of your responsibility to your wife? Why is this truth important?

   _____

2. "Nourish" means to foster growth. What elements of nourishment does your wife need from you to help her grow?

   _____

3. The term "cherish" is from the Greek word meaning "to incubate or brood," and indicates esteeming someone as a priority. How can you show your wife you esteem and value her? Be specific.

   _____

4. One aspect of leadership is bringing appropriate resources to a situation to help others become successful. What resources do you need to use in order to nourish and cherish your wife so she can succeed as a woman, wife and mother (help with her schedule, assist with a problem, give or get direct help with a task, provide encouragement, spend time with her, etc.)?

   _____

HOMEBUILDERS PRINCIPLE FOR MEN #3:

The husband who is becoming a caring head of his house is one who encourages his wife to grow and become all that God intended her to be.

Choose one act of servant-leadership, unselfish loving or caring for your wife which you will share with one other man in our group and for which you will agree to be accountable to the group by the next session.

   _____

Make a date with your mate to meet in the next few days to complete **HomeBuilders Project #10.**

_____   _____   _____
Date   Time   Location

Recommended Reading

Rocking the Roles by Robert Lewis and William Hendricks.

This book provides a balanced, biblical guide to understanding marital roles.

Building Your Mate's Self-Esteem by Dennis and Barbara Rainey.

In this book you will find clues to understanding your wife's self-esteem, laws that will help you to free your mate from her past and building blocks to strengthen her self-esteem.

The Questions Book for Marriage Intimacy by Dennis and Barbara Rainey.

This short book offers 31 questions you've probably never thought to ask your mate. These questions will ignite your curiosity and rekindle your fascination for each other. These questions will spark many memorable hours of sharing, sharpen your understanding of your mate and stimulate closeness in new areas of your marriage.

Staying Close by Dennis Rainey.

Chapter 14—"The Making of a Servant-leader"—elaborates on the material covered in this session.

HomeBuilders Project #10
Husbands

Set aside an hour and a half to complete this project.

1. Review the lesson on the responsibilities of a husband. (Complete any unfinished questions.)

2. Ask God to show you how you are to be the best possible husband for your wife.

3. Make a list of 10 to 15 of your wife's needs, grouping them in the following areas of life (You may wish to schedule a special time to ask her what they really are.):

Physical   Social

_____   _____
_____   _____
_____   _____

Spiritual   Mental

_____   _____
_____   _____
_____   _____

Emotional

_____
_____
_____

4. List three of the above needs which seem to be of greatest importance to her at this time.

_____ _____ _____

5. After verifying these needs with your wife, list appropriate actions you need to take to help meet those needs, demonstrating your desire to be God's man in her life.

_____

6. Pray again, asking God to give you wisdom and skill in meeting your wife's needs effectively.

7. Write your wife's needs on a 3×5-inch card and place it where you will see it daily (mirror, desk drawer, etc.) as a reminder of how you can meet her needs in a practical way.

8. Be prepared to share your successes and/or failures next time. Your responses will encourage others in the group.

Remember to bring your calendar for **Make a Date** to the next class session.

SESSION 10

WIVES

Fitting Together Part Two

OBJECTIVES

You will help the wives learn to fit together with their husbands as you guide them to:

- Identify four biblical responsibilities a wife has to her husband;
- Discuss hurdles that interfere with fulfilling these responsibilities;
- Choose specific actions to fulfill these responsibilities; and
- Commit to being accountable to the other wives in fulfilling these responsibilities.

There are four biblical responsibilities God wants a wife to assume toward her husband: making marriage a priority, unselfish love, submission, and respect.

Student is on page 175.

(10-15 Minutes)

What are some of your struggles in trying to succeed as a wife?

_____

Tip: Point out that it is helpful to admit to one another those areas where we personally find difficulties. Share one or two of your own responses to this question, then listen for indications of women experiencing confusion, pressure or even bitterness about their circumstances. Some may want to vent their frustrations with what they see as their husbands' inadequate leadership. Explain that the focus of this session will not be on pointing out where our husbands are off base, but on discovering specific ways to become successful as a wife.

Comment: "Oneness results when a couple follows God's blueprints, receives one another as God's gift, and then constructs their marriage by leaving parents, cleaving to each other and becoming one flesh."

(65-75 Minutes)

Student is on page 175.

A. The Third Responsibility—Submission
(15-20 Minutes)

At this point of the section you may find it helpful to briefly tell the women some of what their husbands are learning about the concept of "headship." For example, they're learning about the concept of being a "servant-leader" as opposed to a "dictatorial leader." Most arguments against roles in marriage stem from the fact that many men throughout history have been dictatorial leaders of their homes. Servant-leadership, however, may be a new concept to many. Lead the women in responding to the following questions:

1. According to Ephesians 5:22, a wife should demonstrate both an attitude of submission and the actions that result from it. What reactions does the idea of submission generate among women? Why?

_____

Answer: The very word "submission" causes a negative reaction in many women. It conjures up images of a husband ordering his wife around and forcing her to do his will, and the wife meekly responding to his every wish.

2. Why is submission seen as a threat to women?

_____

Answer: Because they feel it demeans their status and puts them in a role of inferiority.

Tip: Some of the answers to Question 1 may also apply to Question 2. After a few minutes of discussion, point out that the biblical view of submission is very different from the common ideas of inferiority, loss of identity or blind obedience that many people assume. Be sure the women notice that the attitude the wife should have toward her husband ("be subject to") is qualified by the phrase, "as to the Lord." This conveys the sense of transferring to the husband the same love and trust given to God.

3. In what areas of marriage do you struggle with submission?

_____

Tip: Share one area of your relationship with your husband in which you struggle with submission. Then invite volunteers to tell of one area of similar struggle in their marriages.

4. What does Scripture say is involved in submission?

Tip: Assign each pair of women one of the Scripture references to read and report on words or phrases that describe something about what submission involves. If you have fewer than five women in the group, be prepared to share the information in the verses not assigned. Allow a minute or two for reading and thinking before calling on women to share what they discovered.

1 Peter 2:21-23

_____

Answer: Jesus set the example for submission by enduring injustice, trusting Himself to God's care.

1 Peter 3:1,2

_____

Answer: Submission demonstrates purity and respect and can influence a husband for good.

1 Peter 3:3,4

_____

Answer: Submission reflects gentleness and is prized by God.

1 Peter 3:5,6

_____

Answer: The wife who submits does not need to fear, for she is doing right.

Titus 2:5

_____

Answer: Submission is part of being sensible, pure and kind—and brings honor to God's Word.

Comment: "Submission comes from two Greek words meaning 'under' and 'arrange or complete.' The sense of the term is to voluntarily organize or fit into or under in a way that makes a complete whole."

Option: Read aloud 1 John 4:18, then ask what submission has to do with the truth that "perfect love casts out fear." (A person who truly loves and is loved by someone will not be afraid to submit—voluntarily fit—to that person.)

5. Why is submission to your husband important...

    Tip: Ask a different woman to respond to each of the parts of Question 5.

    a.   to his leadership?

    _____

    Answer: Willing submission makes it possible for a man to exercise servant-leadership. Assertion or unwillingness forces a man to either become passive, become a manipulator, or become dictatorial.

    b.   to his love for you?

    _____

    Answer: Willing submission makes it easy for a man to exercise unselfish love. Unwillingness tends to encourage response in kind, resulting in isolation and loss of oneness.

    c.   to his care for you?

    _____

    Answer: Submission makes a man more aware of his responsibility to nourish and cherish.

d.   to his trust of you?

_____

Answer: Trust grows in a climate free of competition and selfish desire.

6.   What advice would you give to help a wife submit to a husband…

Tip: Ask for volunteers to suggest advice to help a wife submit to a husband—expect group members to raise some deeply felt concerns. The focus of this discussion should not be trying to identify specific actions that "solve" every situation, but rather to engage group members in a few minutes of envisioning obedient actions and attitudes in difficult situations.

a.   who is *passive* and doesn't lead?

_____

b.   who is a *dictator*, doesn't listen and demands submission?

_____

Tip: Point out that these difficult situations are where most wives encounter their biggest problem in submitting. The natural inclination is to say, "I'll submit when he does his part correctly." While fitting together with someone who pleases us is very agreeable, it is precisely those times when disagreements arise that it is most necessary to respond "as to the Lord," trusting His perfect wisdom and following His example. When a wife allows herself to get into a power struggle with her husband, she risks costing both of them the oneness necessary for their relationship to grow.

CAUTION: Submission does not require a wife to violate other scriptural commands or principles. The Bible does not ask wives to submit to sinful or damaging demands. If the issue of spouse abuse is raised, remind them of these passages that provide wise counsel:

- *Proverbs 14:7 says to "leave the presence of a fool." This does not mean divorce; it simply advises making enough space to avoid the influence of the fool.*
- *Romans 5:8 shares Christ's example of loving the sinner even though hating sin (Psalm 45:7). An abusive husband needs help, not silence.*
- *Romans 13:1 and 1 Peter 2:13-15 teach God's establishment of governmental authority to control those who do wrong. A wife in danger should not hesitate to contact the authorities for protection.*

7. What are two ways (two areas) that you can demonstrate submission to your husband? (Be sure to select areas that would really encourage him, not just the areas that would be easiest for you.)

_____

Tip: Share one or two examples of ways you demonstrate submission to your husband. Instruct each woman to privately write two ways that she can demonstrate submission to her husband.

Summarize this discussion by reading aloud the following principle:

HOMEBUILDERS PRINCIPLE FOR WOMEN #3:

In order for a husband to successfully lead, he must have a wife who willingly submits to his leadership.

B. The Fourth Responsibility—Respect
(20 Minutes)

"And let the wife see that she respects *and* reverences her husband [that she notices him, regards him, honors him, prefers him, venerates, and esteems him; and that she defers to him, praises him, and loves and admires him exceedingly]" (Ephesians 5:33, *AMP N.T.*).

Tip: Have the women work in pairs to write their observations about what the above paragraph says it means for a wife to respect her husband. After a few minutes, ask each pair to share their observations.

1. What are your observations of what this paragraph says it means to respect your husband?

_____

2. Why do men need their wives' respect? Why is respect important to an insecure man? What are some specific reasons that your husband needs your respect?

_____

Answer: Respect builds a man's confidence, his trust and his desire to live up to this admiration.

3. How do you communicate your respect to your husband?

_____

4. Thoughtfully list some additional ways that you can verbally and actively show respect to your husband. (Think back to those times when he has exemplified confidence in his ability as a man.)

VERBALLY	ACTIVELY
1.	1.
2.	2.
3.	3.

Tip: Share one or two of your own answers to questions 3 and 4 to stimulate ideas. Then have women work privately to write their answers to those questions. After a few minutes, ask volunteers to share one answer to Question 3 and one idea from either list in Question 4.

5. Review the four topics you have explored in Session 9 and 10. Choose one thing for which you will be accountable to the group to do before the next session—to make your marriage a priority, to express unselfish love, to willingly submit or to show respect to your husband.

HOMEBUILDERS PRINCIPLE FOR WOMEN #4:
A successful wife is one who respects her husband.

Make a Date

Student is on page 178.

Make a date with your mate to meet in the next few days to complete *HomeBuilders Project #10*. Your leader will ask at the next session for you to share one thing from this experience.

Date	Time	Location

Rejoin the husbands for a few moments to have the couples make a date to complete HomeBuilders Project #10 this week.

   Distribute the HomeBuilders Project pages you duplicated. Point out that this week's project requires between 60 and 90 minutes. There are separate projects for husbands and wives, both of which focus on identifying and meeting each other's needs. Couples should do their projects at the same time so that they can check with each other to see if they have accurately listed each other's needs.

Rocking the Roles by Robert Lewis and William Hendricks.

This book provides a balanced, biblical guide to understanding marital roles.

Building Your Mate's Self-Esteem by Dennis and Barbara Rainey.

In this book you will find clues to understanding your husband's self-esteem, laws that will help you to free your mate from his past and building blocks to strengthen his self-esteem.

The Questions Book for Marriage Intimacy by Dennis and Barbara Rainey.

This short book offers 31 questions you've probably never thought to ask your mate. These questions will ignite your curiosity and rekindle your fascination for each other. These questions will spark many memorable hours of sharing, sharpen your understanding of your mate and stimulate closeness in new areas of your marriage.

Staying Close by Dennis Rainey.

Chapter 15—"How to Love Your Husband" expands on the material discussed in this session.

Conclude the session with prayer. Because of the extended time schedule for this session, it may be too late for people to remain for refreshments and fellowship. Be considerate of people's schedules in making your decision.

SESSION 10

WIVES

Fitting Together Part Two

There are four biblical responsibilities God wants a wife to assume toward her husband: making marriage a priority, unselfish love, submission, and respect.

What are some of your struggles in trying to succeed as a wife?

A. The Third Responsibility—Submission

1. According to Ephesians 5:22, a wife should demonstrate both an attitude of submis-

sion and the actions that result from it. What reactions does the idea of submission generate among women? Why?

_____

2. Why is submission seen as a threat to women?

_____

3. In what areas of marriage do you struggle with submission?

_____

4. What does Scripture say is involved in submission?
   1 Peter 2:21-23

   _____

   1 Peter 3:1,2

   _____

   1 Peter 3:3,4

   _____

   1 Peter 3:5,6

   _____

   Titus 2:5

   _____

5. Why is submission to your husband important...
   a.   to his leadership?

   _____

   b.   to his love for you?

   _____

   c.   to his care for you?

   _____

   d.   to his trust of you?

   _____

6. What advice would you give to help a wife submit to a husband...
   a.   who is **passive** and doesn't lead?

   _____

   b.   who is a **dictator**, doesn't listen and demands submission?

   _____

7. What are two ways (two areas) that you can demonstrate submission to your husband? (Be sure to select areas that would really encourage him, not just the areas that would be easiest for you.)

   _____

HOMEBUILDERS PRINCIPLE FOR WOMEN #3:

In order for a husband to successfully lead, he must have a wife who willingly submits to his leadership.

B. The Fourth Responsibility—Respect

"And let the wife see that she respects *and* reverences her husband [that she notices him, regards him, honors him, prefers him, venerates, and esteems him; and that she defers to him, praises him, and loves and admires him exceedingly]" (Ephesians 5:33, *AMP N.T.*).

1. What are your observations of what this paragraph says it means to respect your husband?

   _____

2. Why do men need their wives' respect? Why is respect important to an insecure man? What are some specific reasons that **your** husband needs **your** respect?

   _____

3. How do you communicate your respect to your husband?

   _____

4. Thoughtfully list some additional ways that you can verbally and actively show respect to your husband. (Think back to those times when he has exemplified confidence in his ability as a man.)

VERBALLY	ACTIVELY
1.	1.
2.	2.
3.	3.

5. Review the four topics you have explored in Session 9 and 10. Choose **one** thing for which you will be accountable to the group to do before the next session—to make your marriage a priority, to express unselfish love, to willingly submit or to show respect to your husband.

HOMEBUILDERS PRINCIPLE FOR WOMEN #4:

A successful wife is one who respects her husband.

Make a Date

Make a date with your mate to meet in the next few days to complete **HomeBuilders Project #10**. Your leader will ask at the next session for you to share one thing from this experience.

_____ _____ _____

Date   Time   Location

Recommended Reading

Rocking the Roles by Robert Lewis and William Hendricks.

This book provides a balanced, biblical guide to understanding marital roles.

Building Your Mate's Self-Esteem by Dennis and Barbara Rainey.

In this book you will find clues to understanding your husband's self-esteem, laws that will help you to free your mate from his past and building blocks to strengthen his self-esteem.

The Questions Book for Marriage Intimacy by Dennis and Barbara Rainey.

This short book offers 31 questions you've probably never thought to ask your mate. These questions will ignite your curiosity and rekindle your fascination for each other. These questions will spark many memorable hours of sharing, sharpen your understanding of your mate and stimulate closeness in new areas of your marriage.

Staying Close by Dennis Rainey.

Chapter 15—"How to Love Your Husband" expands on the material discussed in this session.

HomeBuilders Project #10
Wives

Set aside 60-90 minutes to complete the following project:

1. Review the lesson on the responsibilities of a wife. (Complete any unfinished questions.)

2. Ask God to show you how you are to be the best possible wife for your husband.

3. Make a list of 10 to 15 of your husband's needs, grouping them in the following areas of life (you may wish to schedule a special time to ask him what they really are):

Physical   Social

_____   _____

_____   _____

_____   _____

Spiritual   Mental

_____   _____

_____   _____

_____   _____

Emotional

_____

_____

_____

4. List three of the above needs which seem to be of greatest importance to him at this time.

_____   _____   _____

5. After verifying these needs with your husband, list appropriate actions you need to take to help meet those needs, demonstrating your desire to be God's woman in his life.

_____

6. Pray again, asking God to give you wisdom and skill in meeting your husband's needs effectively.

7. Write your intended actions on a 3×5-inch card and place it where you will see it daily (mirror, purse, etc.) as a reminder of how you can meet his needs in practical ways.

8. Be prepared to share in the next session your successes as well as failures, so that you might encourage others in the group.

Remember to bring your calendar for **Make a Date** to the next session.

Building in the Spirit: Mastering the Flesh

OBJECTIVES

You will help your group members learn to yield to the Spirit as individuals and as couples as you guide them to:

- Contrast a marriage without God and a marriage with God;
- Identify whether their efforts to build a strong marriage are being done in the-flesh or by the power of the Holy Spirit.

COMMENTS

1. Before teaching this session, it will be helpful if you are familiar with these important booklets by Bill Bright (found in **Recommended Reading** for Session 11):
    How to Be Sure You Are a Christian
    How to Experience God's Love and Forgiveness
    How to Be Filled with the Spirit
    How to Walk in the Spirit

2. If anyone in your class has not yet received Christ as Savior, arrange to share Christ individually with him or her before this session.

3. Be prepared to begin the session with the husbands and wives in separate rooms for sharing their experiences in carrying out the actions planned at the previous session. Because this session contains vital concepts to be taught, it will be important to keep your split group's time to 10 minutes. This session needs ample time to be explored properly.

A husband and wife can experience true oneness only
as they live by faith, in the power of the Holy Spirit.

*Student is on
page 191.*

(15-20 Minutes)

*This **Warm Up** moves quickly from reviewing experiences resulting from the previous session
to introducing the current topic. By this point in the study your group should have reached a
healthy level of openness, but some may still need your support and encouragement.*

> **Option:** *Begin this session with the husbands and wives meeting in separate rooms
> for 8 to 10 minutes of sharing how things went in carrying out the actions planned
> during the previous session.*

*Encourage class members to join a small group (up to five or six per group) and ask each other
these questions which you have lettered on the chalkboard, an overhead transparency or a
poster:*

Which of your plans from the previous session do you feel went well?

What did you find was difficult?

How did your mate respond?

What do you think you might do differently this next week?

What do you feel you want to keep on doing?

*After 8 to 10 minutes, have the husbands and wives gather together in one room. Ask them to
respond to these questions:*

1.   Think back to the childhood tale of "The Three Little Pigs." What is the moral of
     the story?

   Answer: Diligence and hard work will win out against life's problems.

2. Compare the lesson of "The Three Little Pigs" with the key point in Jesus' story of the wise and foolish builders (see Matthew 7:24-27). What is similar in the two stories? What is the key difference in the conclusion of each story?

    Answer: Similar: The first two pigs and the foolish man did not build wisely, and their houses collapsed when trouble came. The third pig and the wise man did build wisely, and their houses weathered the trouble that came.

    Different: The story of the pigs infers that personal effort and thought is adequate to overcoming trouble. Jesus' story defines God's Word as the source of wisdom necessary to triumph over adversity and thus succeed.

3. What is the application for your marriage?

    Answer: According to the wisdom of "Three Little Pigs," a husband and wife can build a solid home through careful planning and diligent effort. But according to Jesus' story, hearing and obeying God's Word is essential to building a home that can stand the tests that life brings.

    Tip: Distribute the Session 11 handouts you have duplicated. Refer to the chart reviewing the main points of the first 10 sessions.

We have spent 10 sessions exploring God's blueprints for marriage—and putting them to work. In this session we will begin to discover how God equips and empowers us to succeed in our desire to achieve oneness with our mates and with Him.

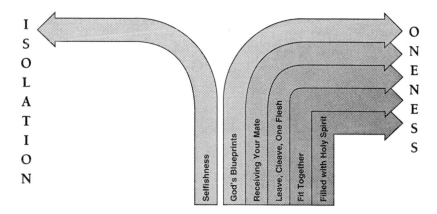

Ask everyone to think silently about what they have learned, and especially about all that is involved in carrying out each of the actions required to build oneness in a marriage.

After a few moments of silence, ask "If you are confident that under all circumstances you and your mate will always be able to carry out all these actions, mark 100 percent in the margin of your handout. If you feel these actions are so totally out of character for you or your mate that you will probably never be able to do any of them, mark 0 percent. Or, estimate a realistic percentage somewhere in between those extremes." Allow a minute or two for people to mark a percentage.

Call for a show of hands of those who marked a figure below 100 percent. "*How about below 90 percent? 80 percent?*" When you get to a number where few people raise their hands, ask "*How many of you would be willing to fly in an airplane with less than an 80 percent chance of landing safely? What does it say to you about our chances for really developing oneness in our marriages if we anticipate a pretty high failure rate in carrying out the actions needed to develop oneness?*"

Allow group members to respond to your questions, then introduce this session by inviting the group to look more closely at the two home builders Jesus talked about.

(30-40 Minutes)

Comment: "*It is impossible to fully cover all the truth regarding the Christian life in one session. The points covered here are intended to encourage individuals and couples to begin to understand the filling of the Holy Spirit as an essential step in a lifelong process of growth.*" (*For further study on this essential topic of Christian living there are some excellent small-group studies available from Campus Crusade for Christ.*)

A. The House the Flesh Builds
(10-15 Minutes)

1. Read Romans 7:18,19. How well do you identify with Paul's lament of his inability to put into practice the truth he believed?

   ❏ I don't have that trouble at all.
   ❏ I fall short occasionally.
   ❏ He said what I feel!
   ❏ I'm even worse off than he was!
   ❏ _____

   Tip: *Ask "How does this problem apply to two individuals who are seeking to build a Christian marriage?" (By themselves they are not capable.)*

Student is on page 192.

2. Scripture frequently shows that even our best human efforts will not only fall short of success, but will actually end in destruction! What are some of the final results of our own desires and efforts ("the deeds of the flesh") as described in Galatians 5:16-21?

_____

Answer: Immorality, impurity, sensuality, idolatry, sorcery, enmities, strife, jealousy, etc.

Option: Ask a follow-up question: "After looking at these gross results, what do you see as the source of our problems in carrying out our good intentions in our lives and marriages?" (The flesh—our sinful nature—keeps us from doing the good things we know we should, for it is in opposition to the purposes of the Spirit [God's blueprints].)

3. How are the "deeds of the flesh" sometimes made evident in your own marriage? (*CAUTION:* Don't embarrass your mate!)

_____

Tip: Share an incident in your marriage when you failed to act on your own good intentions and produced a similarly negative result. Then ask for three or four people in the group to briefly mention a comparable incident—without embarrassing their mates. When the sharing is completed, point out that Paul not only faced these same kinds of situations in his life; he also wrote about the solution to the problems by describing three categories into which all people fit. Instruct everyone to locate 1 Corinthians 2:14—3:3. Read the passage aloud. Briefly explain the three types of people illustrated by the three circles.

4. First Corinthians 2:14—3:3 describes three kinds of people:

 The Natural Person (2:14), who has not received Christ as Savior, does not understand spiritual truth and is in need of spiritual birth;

 The Spiritual Person (2:15,16), who has received Christ and wisely judges or appraises all of life according to God's Word;

 The Worldly or Carnal Person (3:1-3), who has received Christ but has not matured as a Christian and who is trying to live the Christian life by human effort.

Which description best fits you? _____

Tip: Ask everyone to privately write down which description best fits him or her.

185

HOMEBUILDERS PRINCIPLE #8:

Only Spiritual Christians can have a hope of building godly homes.

Important Note! If you sense that anyone in your group is not a Christian, this is a good time to take a few moments to explain the gospel. Refer to "The Four Spiritual Laws" section at the end of this leader's guide.

We suggest that you explain briefly how you can become a Christian and the differences that walking with Christ has made in your life. Then read through The Four Spiritual Laws presentation.

Also included at the end of the leader's guide is a longer explanation of the Holy Spirit and His power in our lives. Suggest to your group members that they read through this on their own.

Student is on page 193.

B. The House the Spirit Builds
(10-15 Minutes)

Comment: Present this brief introduction to the Holy Spirit: "In order for a home to weather the storms of life, its daily builder must be God. Jesus said it was to our advantage that He go to the Father, because He would send God's Holy Spirit (the "Helper" or "Comforter," the Third Person of the Trinity) to lead us, show us His ways and to empower us to represent Him to the world. (See John 14:26.) As two people build a relationship with each other, it is essential that they both yield to the Holy Spirit and allow Him to lead them in every facet of their marriage.

"It is important for us to recognize the Holy Spirit's role in Christian marriage: He is God's personal presence in your marriage." Repeat the statement so each person can write it on the handout.

Option: Ask "Why do you think it is important for God to be present within a marriage?" (The purposes for which God designed marriage cannot be achieved apart from His presence. Intimacy with the Holy Spirit releases God's power in an individual and a marriage. Only He can enable a couple to overcome the barriers to His purpose of oneness.)

1. Read Galatians 5:22-26. This passage identifies the following characteristics of a person (or a home) who is yielding to God's Holy Spirit:

    ❏ Love ❏ Joy ❏ Peace

    ❏ Patience ❏ Kindness ❏ Goodness

    ❏ Faithfulness ❏ Gentleness ❏ Self-Control

    ❏ Not boastful ❏ Not envying ❏ Crucified the flesh

    ❏ Walking by the Spirit ❏ Not challenging (provoking)

    Mark one part of the fruit of the Spirit that you most need in order to create oneness in your marriage.

    How will this quality contribute to oneness in your marriage?

    _____

    Tip: After a minute or two, invite volunteers to share the spiritual quality they checked and to tell how that would contribute to oneness in marriage.

2. Every house has its builder (Hebrews 3:4). Do you feel your home is being built in the energy of the flesh or by the power of the Holy Spirit? Why?

    _____

    If you are to build a godly home (one that shows forth God's character and attributes—His goodness, faithfulness, justice, love, etc.), you must do so through the power that God supplies. Human ability will never achieve godliness. In the previous session we saw the responsibilities for husbands and wives in Ephesians 5:22-31. This passage is preceded by the command to "be filled with the Spirit" (v.18).

3. In what practical everyday situations would the power of the Holy Spirit make a difference in my marriage (i.e., communication, sex, in-laws, roles, conflict resolution, acceptance, etc.)?

    _____

    Comment: Lead the group toward the next segment of this session: "We have seen that the Holy Spirit is an essential ingredient in a life and in a marriage. Yet many feel that living out marriage with the Holy Spirit is confusing or difficult, and they continue to struggle, attempting to build a strong marriage their own ways, not really seeking to submit their lives and their relationships to God's control."

HOMEBUILDERS PRINCIPLE #9:

The home built by God requires both the husband and wife to yield to the Holy Spirit in every area of their lives.

Student is on page 194.

Make a date with your mate to meet in the next few days to complete *HomeBuilders Project #11*. This will aid you as a couple in continuing the process of building your marriage. Your leader will ask at the next session for you to share one thing from this experience.

Date	Time	Location

Tip: Remind the couples to make a date to complete HomeBuilders Project #11 this week. Explain that this project goes in depth about dealing with sin. This project can have a powerful impact on each person's life and marriage and may require additional time to reflect on the issues that are raised.

The Holy Spirit by Bill Bright.

The door to life's greatest adventure—the walk of faith, purpose and power—can be unlocked through the strength and guidance of the Holy Spirit. Find out who He is, His purpose and His relationship to you. These are basic principles for spiritual growth and ministry effectiveness.

Staying Close by Dennis Rainey.

Chapter 13—"The Power for Oneness"—discusses the role of the Holy Spirit in strengthening your marriage.

Transferable Concepts for Powerful Living by Bill Bright.

1. *How to Be Sure You Are a Christian*
2. *How to Experience God's Love and Forgiveness*
3. *How to Be Filled with the Spirit*
4. *How to Walk in the Spirit*

These booklets explain the "how-to's" of consistent, successful Christian living. Excellent for personal enrichment and as gifts for growing Christians.

Conclude with prayer and a time of fellowship.

SESSION 11

Building in the Spirit: Mastering the Flesh

A husband and wife can experience true oneness only as they live by faith, in the power of the Holy Spirit.

1. Think back to the childhood tale of "The Three Little Pigs." What is the moral of the story?

2. Compare the lesson of "The Three Little Pigs" with the key point in Jesus' story of the wise and foolish builders (Matthew 7:24-27). What is similar in the two stories? What is the key difference in the conclusion of each story?

3. What is the application for your marriage?

We have spent 10 sessions exploring God's blueprints for marriage—and putting them to work. In this session we will discover how God equips and empowers us to succeed in our desire to achieve oneness with our mates and with Him.

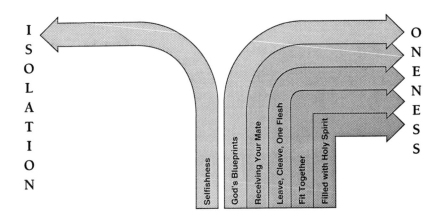

A. The House the Flesh Builds

1. Read Romans 7:18,19. How well do you identify with Paul's lament of his inability to put into practice the truth he believed?

   ❑ I don't have that trouble at all.
   ❑ I fall short occasionally.
   ❑ He said what I feel!
   ❑ I'm even worse off than he was!
   ❑ _____

2. Scripture frequently shows that even our best human efforts will not only fall short of success, but will actually end in destruction! What are some of the final results of our own desires and efforts ("the deeds of the flesh") as described in Galatians 5:16-21?

   _____

3. How are the "deeds of the flesh" sometimes made evident in your own marriage? (CAUTION: Don't embarrass your mate!)

   _____

4. First Corinthians 2:14—3:3 describes three kinds of people:

 The Natural Person (2:14), who has not received Christ as Savior, does not understand spiritual truth and is in need of spiritual birth;

 The Spiritual Person (2:15,16), who has received Christ and wisely judges or appraises all of life according to God's Word;

 The Worldly or Carnal Person (3:1-3), who has received Christ but has not matured as a Christian and who is trying to live the Christian life by human effort.

Which description best fits you? _____

HOMEBUILDERS PRINCIPLE #8:

Only Spiritual Christians can have a hope of building godly homes.

B. The House the Spirit Builds

1. Read Galatians 5:22-26. This passage identifies the following characteristics of a person (or a home) who is yielding to God's Holy Spirit:

   ❑ Love   ❑ Joy   ❑ Peace
   ❑ Patience   ❑ Kindness   ❑ Goodness
   ❑ Faithfulness   ❑ Gentleness   ❑ Self-Control
   ❑ Not boastful   ❑ Not envying   ❑ Crucified the flesh
   ❑ Walking by the Spirit   ❑ Not challenging (provoking)

   Mark one part of the fruit of the Spirit that you most need in order to create oneness in your marriage.

   How will this quality contribute to oneness in your marriage?

   _____

2. Every house has its builder (Hebrews 3:4). Do you feel your home is being built in the energy of the flesh or by the power of the Holy Spirit? Why?

   _____

   If you are to build a godly home (one that shows forth God's character and attributes—His goodness, faithfulness, justice, love, etc.), you must do so through the power that God supplies. Human ability will never achieve godliness. In the previous session we saw the responsibilities for husbands and wives in Ephesians 5:22-31. This passage is preceded by the command to "be filled with the Spirit" (v.18)

3. In what practical everyday situations would the power of the Holy Spirit make a difference in my marriage (i.e., communication, sex, in-laws, roles, conflict resolution, acceptance, etc.)?

HOMEBUILDERS PRINCIPLE #9:

The home built by God requires both the husband and wife to yield to the Holy Spirit in every area of their lives.

Make a date with your mate to meet in the next few days to complete **HomeBuilders Project #11**. This will aid you as a couple in continuing the process of building your marriage. Your leader will ask at the next session for you to share one thing from this experience.

Date	Time	Location

The Holy Spirit by Bill Bright.

The door to life's greatest adventure—the walk of faith, purpose and power—can be unlocked through the strength and guidance of the Holy Spirit. Find out who He is, His purpose and His relationship to you. These are basic principles for spiritual growth and ministry effectiveness.

Staying Close by Dennis Rainey.

Chapter 13—"The Power for Oneness"—discusses the role of the Holy Spirit in strengthening your marriage.

Transferable Concepts for Powerful Living by Bill Bright.

1. *How to Be Sure You Are a Christian*
2. *How to Experience God's Love and Forgiveness*
3. *How to Be Filled with the Spirit*
4. *How to Walk in the Spirit*

These booklets explain the "how-to's" of consistent, successful Christian living. Excellent for personal enrichment and as gifts for growing Christians.

Learning to live the Christian life is an ongoing process. The following project will aid you in your discovery of God's forgiveness. Building a home that reflects God's character is a matter of choices—choices that are made by faith, trusting that God's Word is true and that He will do what He promises in Scripture.

As a Couple: 5 Minutes

Share with each other two or three things that really spoke to your needs from Session 11.

Individually: 20 Minutes

A. We Must Desire to Walk in the Spirit

1. What does Matthew 5:6 teach about a prerequisite for walking in the power of the Holy Spirit?

    _____

2. Why is the desire to be Christlike so important?

    _____

3. Proverbs 2:1-5 speaks of a commitment to and desire for knowing God. List applications to your marriage that you can discern from this passage.

    _____

B. We Must Continually Confess Our Sin

1. Sin plagues us in our relationship with God. It alienates us from Him (Proverbs 15:9) and produces "death" (Romans 6:23). Since sin breaks our fellowship with God, it is necessary to restore that relationship when we find that we have been displeasing Him. What does the Bible say to do when fellowship with God has been broken (1 John 1:5-10)?

    _____

2. To confess means "to agree with another." We agree with God that our actions or attitudes are wrong. We then repent, turning from these sins and back to God, thanking Him for Christ's death on the cross for all our sins. Why is repentance crucial to our confession?

    _____

3. Read Colossians 2:13,14. When we confess our sin before God, should we...
    - ❑ beg for God's forgiveness?
    - ❑ thank Him that the penalty has been paid and that He has already forgiven us?

Note: An exercise that hundreds of thousands of Christians have found meaningful is to take a separate sheet of paper and spend time alone with God, asking Him to reveal any sin that is unconfessed before Him. The following steps are recommended:

1. Title the page, "For God's Eyes Only." Prayerfully list on the page actions and attitudes that are contrary to God's Word and purposes. Focus on areas that affect your mate.

2. Write the words of 1 John 1:9 across your list of sins, thanking God for His absolute forgiveness of all that you have done in the past, present and future. Thank Him for sending His Son to the cross to die for your sins.

3. It may be necessary and appropriate for you to also confess to your mate any attitudes or actions that have been harmful to him/her. Caution: Do not dredge up something from the past that would be more than your mate can handle. Seek wise counsel and avoid dropping any "atomic bombs." There is a significant difference between confessing something that your mate knows about and "getting something off your chest" that makes you feel better but becomes a severe problem to your mate.

4. Destroy the page and continue your study on being filled with the Holy Spirit.

4. When you are tempted to sin, what does God's Word promise in 1 Corinthians 10:13?

_____

5. As a Christian, you have power over sin. Read Romans 6:1-18 and answer the following questions:
   a. What happened to your sinful nature when you received Christ (v. 6)?

   _____

   b. According to verse 11, what must you do?

   _____

   c. According to verses 16 and 17, what choices must you make?

   _____

   d. Have you been freed from sin?   ❑ Yes   ❑ No
      Are you still a slave to sin?   ❑ Yes   ❑ No
      To what are you to be a slave?

   _____

   e. What do you need to do as a result of studying these verses about the freedom Christ has given you?

   _____

Interact as a Couple: 10-15 Minutes

Share with one another the decision you have made in response to this study. Your relationship with one another will benefit as you openly talk about your spiritual commitments—as well as confiding any questions or struggles. Close your time together by praying for one another.

Remember to bring your calendar for **Make a Date** to the next session.

SESSION 12

Building in the Spirit: Being Filled

OBJECTIVES

You will help your group members learn to yield to the Spirit as individuals and couples as you guide them to:

- Discuss ways an individual and a couple can restore and maintain a relationship with the Spirit; and
- Pray by faith to confess known sin and to ask for the Spirit's filling.

COMMENTS

1. As with preparing to teach Session 11, make sure you are familiar with these important booklets by Bill Bright (found in **Recommended Reading**):
    How to Be Sure You Are a Christian
    How to Experience God's Love and Forgiveness
    How to Be Filled with the Spirit
    How to Walk in the Spirit

2. Before the session, plan for you and your spouse (and or any other appropriate class members) to call each person in the class and inquire about any questions they have about the content of Session 11. Ask "Is there a specific area related to the Holy Spirit that I could be praying about with you?" Show your concern and be sensitive to people's spiritual struggles.

3. **Option:** Consider arranging for a group member—or your mate—to share briefly about the Holy Spirit's ministry in his or her life and marriage. Meet with this person ahead of time to review what will be shared, making sure it will be brief, practical and supportive of the concepts in the above booklets.

A husband and wife can experience true oneness only
as they live by faith, in the power of the Holy Spirit.

*Student is on
page 207.*

(10-15 Minutes)

*This **Warm Up** reviews the previous session and introduces the current session topic. Be sensitive to individuals who may need your support and encouragement in considering their spiritual conditions.*

On the chalkboard, an overhead transparency or a large poster mounted at the front of the room, letter the text of 1 John 1:9. On another poster, mounted at the back of the room, letter these two equations:

- *Sin = Punishment*
- *Sin + Confession = Forgiveness + Cleansing*

As people arrive, have them form groups of no more than five or six per group. Call their attention to the text of 1 John 1:9 and the two equations. Ask for a show of hands of those who completed HomeBuilders Project #11.

Tell about a time when you experienced forgiveness, either from God or from another person. Then ask each person, starting with the one in each group who has gone the longest without fixing breakfast for his or her mate, to tell about a time when he or she experienced forgiveness.

Comment: "Last week we began exploring the ways in which the Holy Spirit works within our lives, both for our personal and spiritual well-being and also to make a positive difference in our marriages. In this session we will continue to discover how the Holy Spirit equips and empowers us to succeed in our desire to achieve oneness with our mates and with Him."

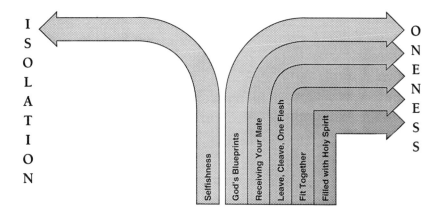

Student is on page 208.

(35-45 Minutes)

Comment: "This session is intended to encourage individuals and couples to begin to experience the filling of the Holy Spirit as an essential step in a lifelong process of growth." (For further study on this essential topic of Christian living there are some excellent small-group studies available from Campus Crusade for Christ.)

Distribute the Session 12 handouts you have duplicated.

A. The Holy Spirit in Your Life
(20-25 Minutes)

1. Read Ephesians 5:18. Paul contrasts being "filled with the Spirit" with being "drunk with wine." What does this comparison say to you about what it means to be filled with the Spirit?

_____

Answer: This imagery conveys the idea of being controlled and empowered.

To be filled (controlled and empowered) by the Holy Spirit is a process that will be repeated many times as you yield yourself to Christ and His authority over your life. It literally means "keep on being filled."

Option: If you contacted someone earlier in the week about sharing his or her experience with being filled with the Spirit, this would be a good time to have him or her talk.

2. How then can you be filled with the Holy Spirit? The following are some beginning steps. (This process is further developed in the *HomeBuilders Project* to be done after this session.)

    a. God will not fill an unclean vessel. What does 1 John 1:9 tell us to do about the sin in our lives? What does it mean to do this?

    _____

    Answer: Confess it. Confession means to agree or admit that something is true. Confessing our sin involves telling God that we have sinned against Him. We must recognize that any relationship is damaged by selfishness (sin) in either partner. Oneness can only grow when selfishness is confronted and dealt with. When we sin, oneness with God is broken and must be dealt with before fellowship can be renewed.

    b. Knowing that we receive Christ by faith, how then do we allow Him to control our lives moment by moment? (Colossians 2:6)

    _____

    Answer: The same way as we received Him—by faith. The phrase "walking in the Spirit" refers to the range of activities of an individual's life, conveying the idea of trusting daily in the power of the Spirit in contrast to depending on even the best of human intentions.

    c. What is faith and why is it important in being filled with the Spirit? (Hebrews 11:1,6)

    _____

    Answer: Faith is assurance that something—or Someone—is true, no matter what we feel or what the circumstances are. Without faith in God we cannot please Him, for then we are depending on ourselves or some other source rather than on Him and His Word. We exercise faith when we trustingly yield control of our lives to Him, rather than trying to succeed through our own best efforts. While feelings are usually involved, they are not the basis for assurance, since they are so easily changed by circumstances.

    d. Does God desire to fill you with His Holy Spirit? (Ephesians 5:18)

    _____

Answer: He would only command us to be filled with the Spirit if He desired it for us.

e. What has God promised you? (1 John 5:14,15)

_____

Answer: God promises in His Word to answer any request that is in accord with His will. Since He has specifically stated that it is His will to fill us with His Spirit, you can be assured that if you pray for Him to fill you, He will honor your prayer.

 The Natural Person (2:14), who has not received Christ as Savior, does not understand spiritual truth and is in need of spiritual birth;

 The Spiritual Person (2:15,16), who has received Christ and wisely judges or appraises all of life according to God's Word;

 The Worldly or Carnal Person (3:1-3), who has received Christ but has not matured as a Christian and who is trying to live the Christian life by human effort.

Which description best fits you? _____

f.   Look again at the three circles we considered in the previous session. Which one represents your life now?

_____

   Which one do you want to represent your life?

_____

Tip: Briefly review the explanation for the three circles which were studied in the previous session. Then ask each person to privately write his or her answers to the two questions.

Comment: "This session has established several essential facts about being filled with the Holy Spirit:

- *It is a command.*
- *It is a promise God will honor.*
- It is essential in building a life and a marriage upon the Rock, able to withstand life's onslaughts.

g.   After considering these truths, once again distinguish the difference between the wise man and foolish man in Matthew 7:24-27.

_____

Answer: In the previous session, we compared Jesus' description of the wise builder with the third little pig in the children's story. We saw that the pig was depending on his own planning and effort; the wise builder was listening to and obeying God's Word.

   h.   What steps do you need to take to insure that your house is being built upon the Rock?

_____

Answer: Confess your sin. In faith yield your life to His control instead of your own control. Ask Him to fill you with His Spirit. Obey God and His Word.

   i.   Will you ask God to fill you and control you with His Spirit?

_____

Tip: Ask each person to privately write his or her answer.

   j.   Why not take a moment right now and bow in prayer, asking God to empower you with His Spirit?

Tip: Ask the class to spend a minute or two in silent prayer. Allow 60-90 seconds for this process. Do not be afraid of the silence—it is a time of evaluation and, most importantly, response to God.

3.   If you confessed your sins, yielded your life to Him and asked God to fill you with His Spirit, then did He fill you with His Spirit? How can you know?

_____

Answer: Yes. Refer back to God's statement of His will in Ephesians 5:18 and His promise to grant requests which are in accord with His will. Faith in His integrity and His Word is the basis for our assurance.

Student is on page 209.

B. The Holy Spirit Makes a Difference
(15-20 Minutes)

1.   In what practical everyday situations would the power of the Holy Spirit make a difference in my marriage (i.e., communication, sex, in-laws, roles, conflict resolution, acceptance, etc.)?

_____

Tip: Be prepared to share one or more examples from your own marriage of how the Holy Spirit has made a positive difference in your relationship with your mate.

2.   What one thing can I do to see this difference realized?

_____

Tip: Instruct participants to privately write an answer to Question 2. Allow two or three minute for people to think and write. When the two or three minutes are up, invite volunteers to share the answer they wrote as a way of helping each other think of actions to take.

Summarize this sharing by again reminding the class of these central points about the Christian life:

- *Walking in the Holy Spirit is by faith, not feelings.*
- *Walking in the Holy Spirit is a subjective experience which is objectified (confirmed) by the Word of God.*
- *Walking in the Holy Spirit requires a sensitive and submissive spirit, continually yielding control to Him.*

Student is on page 209.

Make a date with your mate to meet in the next few days to complete *HomeBuilders Project #12*. This will aid you as a couple in continuing the process of building your marriage. Your leader will ask at the next session for you to share one thing from this experience.

| _____ | _____ | _____ |
| Date | Time | Location |

Tip: Remind the couples to make a date to complete HomeBuilders Project #12 this week. Explain that this project goes more in depth about being filled with the Spirit and can have significant impact on each person's life and marriage. As with last week's project, this one may take a little longer than usual.

The Holy Spirit by Bill Bright.

The door to life's greatest adventure—the walk of faith, purpose and power—can be unlocked through the strength and guidance of the Holy Spirit. Find out who He is, His purpose and His relationship to you. These are basic principles for spiritual growth and ministry effectiveness.

Staying Close by Dennis Rainey.

Chapter 13—"The Power for Oneness"—discusses the role of the Holy Spirit in strengthening your marriage.

Transferable Concepts for Powerful Living by Bill Bright.

1. *How to Be Sure You Are a Christian*
2. *How to Experience God's Love and Forgiveness*
3. *How to Be Filled with the Spirit*
4. *How to Walk in the Spirit*

These booklets explain the "how-to's" of consistent, successful Christian living. Excellent for personal enrichment and as gifts for growing Christians.

Conclude with prayer and a time of fellowship.

SESSION 12

Building in the Spirit: Being Filled

A husband and wife can experience true oneness only as they live by faith, in the power of the Holy Spirit.

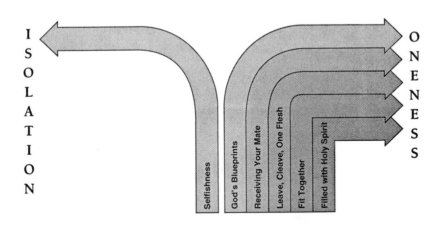

ISOLATION

Selfishness

God's Blueprints

Receiving Your Mate

Leave, Cleave, One Flesh

Fit Together

Filled with Holy Spirit

ONENESS

A. The Holy Spirit in Your Life

1. Read Ephesians 5:18. Paul contrasts being "filled with the Spirit" with being "drunk with wine." What does this comparison say to you about what it means to be filled with the Spirit?

   _____

   To be filled (controlled and empowered) by the Holy Spirit is a process that will be repeated many times as you yield yourself to Christ and His authority over your life. It literally means "keep on being filled."

2. How then can you be filled with the Holy Spirit? The following are some beginning steps. (This process is further developed in the **HomeBuilders Project** to be done after this session.)

   a. God will not fill an unclean vessel. What does 1 John 1:9 tell us to do about the sin in our lives? What does it mean to do this?

   _____

   b. Knowing that we receive Christ by faith, how then do we allow Him to control our lives moment by moment? (Colossians 2:6)

   _____

   c. What is faith and why is it important in being filled with the Spirit? (Hebrews 11:1,6)

   _____

   d. Does God desire to fill you with His Holy Spirit? (Ephesians 5:18)

   _____

   e. What has God promised you? (1 John 5:14,15)

   _____

 The Natural Person (2:14), who has not received Christ as Savior, does not understand spiritual truth and is in need of spiritual birth;

 The Spiritual Person (2:15,16), who has received Christ and wisely judges or appraises all of life according to God's Word;

 The Worldly or Carnal Person (3:1-3), who has received Christ but has not matured as a Christian and who is trying to live the Christian life by human effort.

Which description best fits you? _____

f. Look again at the three circles we considered in the previous session. Which one represents your life now?

_____

Which one do you want to represent your life?

_____

g. After considering these truths, once again distinguish the difference between the wise man and foolish man in Matthew 7:24-27.

_____

h. What steps do you need to take to insure that your house is being built upon the Rock?

_____

i. Will you ask God to fill you and control you with His Spirit?

_____

j. Why not take a moment right now and bow in prayer, asking God to empower you with His Spirit?

3. If you confessed your sins, yielded your life to Him and asked God to fill you with His Spirit, then did He fill you with His Spirit? How can you know?

_____

B. The Holy Spirit Makes a Difference

1. In what practical, everyday situations would the power of the Holy Spirit make a difference in my marriage (i.e., communication, sex, in-laws, roles, conflict resolution, acceptance, etc.)?

_____

2. What one thing can I do to see this difference realized?

_____

Make a date with your mate to meet in the next few days to complete **HomeBuilders Project #12**. This will aid you as a couple in continuing the process of building your marriage. Your leader will ask at the next session for you to share one thing from this experience.

_____   _____   _____

Date   Time   Location

Recommended Reading

The Holy Spirit by Bill Bright.

The door to life's greatest adventure—the walk of faith, purpose and power—can be unlocked through the strength and guidance of the Holy Spirit. Find out who He is, His purpose and His relationship to you. These are basic principles for spiritual growth and ministry effectiveness.

Staying Close by Dennis Rainey.

Chapter 13—"The Power for Oneness"—discusses the role of the Holy Spirit in strengthening your marriage.

Transferable Concepts for Powerful Living by Bill Bright.

1. *How to Be Sure You Are a Christian*
2. *How to Experience God's Love and Forgiveness*
3. *How to Be Filled with the Spirit*
4. *How to Walk in the Spirit*

These booklets explain the "how-to's" of consistent, successful Christian living. Excellent for personal enrichment and as gifts for growing Christians.

HomeBuilders Project #12

Learning to live the Christian life is an ongoing process. The following project will aid you in your discovery of the great adventures of daily walking in the power of the Holy Spirit. Remember, keep trusting that God's Word is true and that He will do what He promises in Scripture.

As a Couple: 5-10 Minutes
Share with each other two or three things that really spoke to your needs from Session 12.

Individually: 15-20 Minutes

A. We Must Yield Ownership of Our Lives to Jesus Christ
1.   What do Romans 6:12-14; 12:1,2 tell you to do?

_____

2.   Have you ever given Jesus Christ complete ownership of your life?

                                      ❑ Yes   ❑ No

     If not, would you like to right now?   ❑ Yes   ❑ No

Simply bow in prayer and acknowledge His authority over your life. Give Him the "title deed." Write out your commitment to Him in the space below. Sign and date your statement.

_____

_____

_____ Signature _____ Date

B. We Must by Faith Claim the Filling of the Holy Spirit
1.   Check each statement as you read:
    ❑ **His Command:** Be filled with the Spirit (Ephesians 5:18).
    ❑ **His Promise:** He will always answer when we pray according to His will (1 John 5:14,15).
2.   Is it God's will that you be filled with the Holy Spirit?
    ❑ Yes   ❑ No   (Review #1 if you are not sure.)
3.   When you pray in faith and ask God to fill you, will He do it?
    ❑ Yes   ❑ No

How do you know? (Check #1 again.) _____

_____

4.   Why not express right now your obedience and faith to God?

Dear Father, I need You. I admit that I have been directing my own life and I have sinned against You. I thank You that You have forgiven my sins through Christ's death on the cross for me. I now invite Christ to be Lord over all my life. Fill me with the Holy Spirit as You commanded me to be filled, and as You promised in your Word that You would do if I ask in faith. As an expression of my faith, I now thank You for directing my life and for filling me with the Holy Spirit. Amen.

If this prayer expressed the desire of your heart, then simply bow in prayer and trust God to empower you with the Holy Spirit **right now**.

Interact as a Couple: 10-15 Minutes

Share with one another the decision you have made in response to this study. Your relationship with one another will benefit as you openly talk about your spiritual commitments—as well as confiding any questions or struggles. Close your time together by praying for one another.

Be ready to share with the class one specific experience from this project—perhaps an instance when you allowed the Holy Spirit to fill you in your marriage relationship or one area in which you have recognized a struggle in yielding to His control.

Remember to bring your calendar for **Make a Date** to the next session.

Building a Legacy: Influencing Future Generations

OBJECTIVES

You will help your group members build an eternal legacy as you guide them to:

- Compare a worldly legacy with a godly legacy; and
- Identify the spiritual and physical legacies a marriage can leave.

COMMENTS

1. It is crucial that you approach these last two sessions as opportunities to encourage couples to take specific steps beyond this study to keep their marriages growing. While this study has great value in itself, people are likely to gradually return to their previous patterns of living unless they commit to a plan for carrying on the progress made. Continuing effort is required for people to initiate and maintain new directions in their marriages.

    FamilyLife of Campus Crusade for Christ is committed to changing the destiny of the family and providing quality resources to build distinctively Christian marriages. **The HomeBuilders Couples Series®** is designed to take a couple through essential components important to building committed Christian marriages and Christian families.

    Building Teamwork in Your Marriage—Designed for men and women to explore God's purpose for their lives, their roles, responsibilities and differentness.

    Building Your Marriage—The basic introduction of God's principles for marriage.

Building Your Mate's Self-Esteem—A unique plan of building blocks to strengthen your mate's self-image.

Expressing Love in Your Marriage—Designed to show couples God's plan for their love life by seeking God's best for their mates and by being in right relationship with Him.

Growing Together in Christ—As couples discover all the power and joy they can find together in Christ, they will also grow closer to one another.

Life Choices for a Lasting Marriage—Couples learn key, foundational commitments that will guide them closer to God and each other as they make everyday decisions that shape their lives and marriage.

Managing Pressure in Your Marriage—This study will help couples learn how to make better choices, plan for the future and find new solutions as they navigate through the stresses and pressures of life.

Mastering Money in Your Marriage—Developed to help couples identify and grapple with the whole concept of a biblical approach to finances and to provide practical guidelines in planning personal finances.

Resolving Conflict in Your Marriage—Couples can't avoid conflict in marriage but they can learn to handle their conflicts in a way that brings them together instead of driving them further apart.

As you prepare this session, prayerfully consider challenging the couples in your class to either participate in another study, such as *Building Your Mate's Self-Esteem* or begin their own group of couples to study *Building Your Marriage*.

2. If your class includes childless couples, focus most of your attention during this session on spiritual descendants rather than physical descendants. Also, if there are couples whose children are grown or nearly grown and who are not serving Christ, encourage those parents that God is still able to overrule any mistakes made in earlier years. He can use parents' past failures for His good. Encourage these parents to confess their errors to God—and to their children; this can be a powerful means of restoring relationships and communication. Urge them to focus on the remaining

years to use every teachable moment with their children to share their present values and relationships with Christ.

God's purpose for marriage goes beyond intimacy, sharing romantic times together and achieving oneness. Marriage is meant to be a couple's locking arms together to influence their world and future generations with the gospel of Jesus Christ.

Student is on page 223.

(15-20 Minutes)

As people arrive, have them form groups of no more than five or six per group. Distribute the Session 13 handouts you duplicated.

Ask how many did the HomeBuilders Project from the previous session. Ask for a show of hands of those who did the project. Have two people share (for continued accountability) one insight gained from the project.

Read aloud the statements under item #1 and instruct participants to select one.

We have been exposed to much about God's plan for our marriages so far in our study.

1. Mark the concept that you have found to be most significant in your marriage.

    ❑ We must deal with the threats to oneness that result in isolation.
    ❑ We must understand God's blueprints as shown in five purposes for marriage (Mirror, Multiply, Manage, Mutually Complete, Model).
    ❑ We build a solid foundation by receiving our mates as a gift from God.
    ❑ We construct according to God's plan when we leave, cleave and become one flesh, resulting in total transparency with our mates.
    ❑ We fit together with our mates when we commit to fulfilling our roles defined in the blueprint of Scripture.
    ❑ We are empowered by the Holy Spirit to carry out these principles and purposes.

Tip: Call for a show of hands of any who marked the first statement (We must deal with the threats to oneness that result in isolation). Ask those who raise their hands to tell what they have found to be significant in that concept. Continue similarly with the other statements listed.

Tip: Ask people to return to their small groups and share their responses to Question 2, starting with the person in each group who has most recently taken out the garbage at home. Share your own answer to set an example of openness about specific changes in actions or attitudes. Stating these changes in front of the group will help to solidify them in people's minds as important things to continue.

2.   **What do you feel is the most important change you have made thus far in your marriage as a result of this study?**

_____

Note: The answers to Point 1 may touch on Question 2.

Tip: Call attention to the chart contrasting Isolation and Oneness. Alert the class that you are going to read aloud the paragraphs which follow. Assign the people on one side of the room to look for one statement with which they agree and underline it. Assign those on the other side to think of one question these paragraphs raise and write it in the margin.

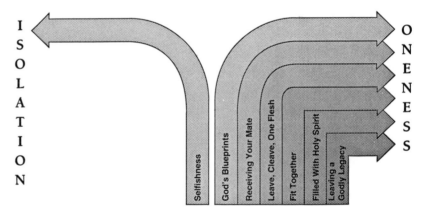

We have learned many things about how to let the Lord build our house. Now we need to learn that "building the house" is not an end in itself.

Although God is deeply interested in our fulfillment as individuals within marriage, He does not give us a "great and satisfying" marriage just so we can have a warm and wonderful relationship with another person. Scripture teaches that in marriage we are to experience growth and acceptance in order to enable us to reach beyond the doors of our home to a neighborhood and a world in great need.

God's heart of love is virtually breaking over people who have not yet received His forgiveness through His Son Jesus Christ. Reconciling people to Himself is God's desire for every individual and for every marriage. You and your mate and those you influence for Christ, including your children, are all a part of God's purpose for planet Earth.

We have already seen that oneness with God and with our mates is necessary for overcoming isolation in our marriages. The oneness we are establishing in our homes is also enabling us to reach out to others afflicted by isolation.

A couple that is working together to meet needs beyond their own front door will leave a spiritual legacy that will outlive them. In so doing, they will discover that their marriage is thriving as they give their lives away in ministering to the needs of others. *Ask for volunteers who underlined a statement with which they agreed to read that statement aloud and tell why they agree with it. After several people have responded, invite those on the other side of the room to share any questions which these paragraphs raised. Write those questions on the chalkboard or an overhead transparency. Encourage people to keep those questions in mind as you proceed to explore the issue of leaving a legacy.*

HOMEBUILDERS PRINCIPLE #10:

The heritage you were handed is not as important as the legacy you will leave.

Student is on page 225.

(30-40 Minutes)

A. Understanding Our Heritage *(10-15 Minutes)*
Lead the class in responding to each of the following questions.

1. What comes to mind when you think of a "heritage" or a "legacy?"

    _____

    Answer: Something that is passed on from one person to another, an inheritance, birthright, etc.

2. There are other types of legacies that people leave. List as many different kinds as you can.

    _____   _____

    Tip: Allow a minute for group members to write, then ask for answers.

3. To what extent is the legacy a person leaves a statement of his or her true values? Explain why this would be so.

_____

Answer: That which outlives a person defines to others what that person really valued.

4. Describe the heritage your parents left to you and the values it represents.

_____

Tip: Briefly share your answer. Then give your class members time to think of their answers and write down some notes to describe the heritage they received. Invite volunteers to read aloud what they have written. Allow plenty of time for sharing here.

5. Look up the following Scriptures and write down words or phrases that describe the legacy God desires you to leave:
   Deuteronomy 6:1,2,5-7

_____

Answer: Fear the Lord, keep His laws, love the Lord, know His Word.

Joshua 24:14,15

_____

Answer: Family commitment to fear and serve God.
Psalm 112:1,2

_____

Answer: Fear the Lord and delight in His commands.
Proverbs 4:10-15

_____

Answer: Wisdom, uprightness.
2 Timothy 1:5

_____

Answer: Sincere faith.
3 John 4

_____

Answer: Walking in the truth.

Tip: Have people return to the small groups in which they began the session. Assign each group one or two of the Scriptures listed. Allow two or three minutes for groups to read and talk, then invite volunteers from each group to share their insights.

Leaving a godly legacy will ultimately be different for every individual. The true test in leaving a godly legacy is an individual's or a couple's faithful fulfillment of God's mission through the stewardship of time, talents and treasure. A godly legacy can be partially measured in the character of the descendants who have been spiritually influenced by a person's life.

HOMEBUILDERS PRINCIPLE #11:
The legacy you leave is determined by the life you live.

B. How to Leave a Legacy That Will Outlive You
(10-15 Minutes)

Student is on page 226.

Have the group look up those two verses to see what they have to say about leaving spiritual descendants:

According to 2 Timothy 2:2 and Psalm 78:3-8, you can leave spiritual as well as physical descendants.

Answer: Second Timothy 2:2 stresses the importance of finding faithful people to build your life into, with the goal of helping them do the same with others who will be faithful.

Psalm 78:3-8 talks about teaching our children about the things of God.

Tip: Ask half of the class to find the answer to Question 1, while the rest of the class explores Question 2. After two or three minutes, invite volunteers to share what they discovered.

1. Read Matthew 28:19,20. How do you leave a spiritual legacy?

    _____

    Answer: By reaching out to those in our world in order to make disciples.

2. According to Deuteronomy 6:4-9, how do you leave a godly legacy through your influence on your children, your physical descendants?

    _____

    Answer: A godly legacy is obviously more than just physical reproduction. God's purpose is not just more people, but to "multiply a godly legacy." Deuteronomy 6 shows that this is accomplished as parents tell and show God's truth to their children in the midst of everyday living.

Tip: Have someone read aloud the story of Henrietta Mears: a classic example of leaving a spiritual legacy.

AN EXAMPLE OF LEAVING A SPIRITUAL LEGACY

As you near the completion of this study, you have become part of the godly legacy from a remarkable single woman who left no physical descendants. Humanly speaking, this study might never have been created if it had not been that Dr. Henrietta Mears befriended a young couple in the early years of their spiritual growth. Bill Bright, founder of Campus Crusade for Christ, and his wife Vonette were strongly influenced by Dr. Mears.

Many other individuals and organizations are part of the spiritual legacy left by Dr. Mears, including Billy Graham, Richard Halverson (former Chaplain of the United States Senate), Gospel Light Publications (a major producer of Bible study resources and Christian literature), Forest Home (one of the largest Christian conference centers in the United States), and Gospel Literature International (GLINT—a service organization aiding in the translation of Christian literature throughout the world).

If you have grown spiritually through this study, then you are a part of the spiritual legacy of Henrietta Mears. Do you believe that God could still be multiplying your spiritual legacy three generations from now?

Comment: "All of us, especially those who are parents, need to be aware that the results of faithful teaching cannot always be seen at present. However, we can know if we are being faithful in sharing our faith and teaching our children, and we can tell if we are growing in our ability to communicate our faith. Children are messengers we send to a time we cannot see—and no project a couple undertakes has more potential for long range impact than faithfully teaching God's truth to their own children."

HOMEBUILDERS PRINCIPLE #12:

Your marriage should leave a legacy of love that will influence future generations.

Student is on page 226.

C. Thinking of My Legacy
(10 Minutes)

These questions push individuals to think about the legacies they want to pass on. This will require more time than the session allows. Therefore, couples will continue this process when they work on the HomeBuilders Project.

Before you have people write answers to these questions, briefly share your response to one or two items, giving group members an idea of how to proceed.

As people write, be available to answer questions and to periodically announce how much time is left.

Allow time to conclude the session by inviting everyone to share within their small groups their responses to one item.

1. What do you want your legacy to be?

2. What people do you need to influence for God?

3. What are some tasks in your church you are gifted to tackle?

4. What project should you support?

Student is on page 227.

Make a date with your mate this week to complete the last *HomeBuilders Project.*

| _____ | _____ | _____ |
| Date | Time | Location |

Remind the couples to make a date to complete HomeBuilders Project #13.

Staying Close by Dennis Rainey

"A Mother's Influence," "A Word to Dads," "Your Family Can Make the Difference," and "How to Become a HomeBuilder" are recommended chapters for this session.

Dream Big: The Henrietta Mears Story edited by Earl Roe.

Lead the group in a time of prayer for each other's continued growth in oneness.

Invite the group to remain for refreshments.

SESSION 13

Building a Legacy: Influencing Future Generations

God's purpose for marriage goes beyond intimacy, sharing romantic times together and achieving oneness. Marriage is meant to be a couple's locking arms together to influence their world and future generations with the gospel of Jesus Christ.

We have been exposed to much about God's plan for our marriages so far in our study.

1. Mark the concept that you have found to be most significant in your marriage:

    ❑ We must deal with the threats to oneness that result in isolation.
    ❑ We must understand God's blueprints as shown in five purposes for marriage (Mirror, Multiply, Manage, Mutually Complete, Model).
    ❑ We build a solid foundation by receiving our mates as a gift from God.
    ❑ We construct according to God's plan when we leave, cleave and become one flesh, resulting in total transparency with our mates.

❑ We fit together with our mates when we commit to fulfilling our roles defined in the blueprint of Scripture.

❑ We are empowered by the Holy Spirit to carry out these principles and purposes.

2. What do you feel is the most important change you have made thus far in your marriage as a result of this study?

_____

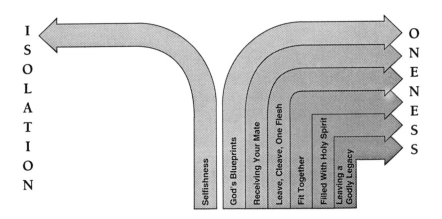

We have learned many things about how to let the Lord build our house. Now we need to learn that "building the house" is not an end in itself.

Although God is deeply interested in our fulfillment as individuals within marriage, He does not give us a "great and satisfying" marriage just so we can have a warm and wonderful relationship with another person. Scripture teaches that in marriage we are to experience growth and acceptance in order to enable us to reach beyond the doors of our homes to a neighborhood and a world in great need.

God's heart of love is virtually breaking over people who have not yet received His forgiveness through His Son Jesus Christ. Reconciling people to Himself is God's desire for every individual and for every marriage. You and your mate and those you influence for Christ, including your children, are all a part of God's purpose for planet Earth.

We have already seen that oneness with God and with our mates is necessary for overcoming isolation in our marriages. The oneness we are establishing in our homes is also enabling us to reach out to others afflicted by isolation.

A couple that is working together to meet needs beyond their own front door will leave a spiritual legacy that will outlive them. In so doing, they will discover that their marriage is thriving as they give their lives away in ministering to the needs of others.

HOMEBUILDERS PRINCIPLE #10:
The heritage you were handed is not as important as the legacy you will leave.

A. Understanding Our Heritage

1. What comes to mind when you think of a "heritage" or a "legacy"?

   _____

2. There are other types of legacies which people leave. List as many different kinds as you can.

   _____

3. To what extent is the legacy a person leaves a statement of his or her true values? Explain why this would be so.

   _____

4. Describe the heritage your parents left to you and the values it represents.

   _____

5. Look up the following Scriptures and write down words or phrases that describe the legacy God desires you to leave:
   Deuteronomy 6:1,2,5-7

   _____

   Joshua 24:14,15

   _____

   Psalm 112:1,2

   _____

   Proverbs 4:10-15

   _____

   2 Timothy 1:5

   _____

   3 John 4

   _____

Leaving a godly legacy will ultimately be different for every individual. The true test in leaving a godly legacy is an individual's or a couple's faithful fulfillment of God's mission through the stewardship of time, talents and treasure. A godly legacy can be partially measured in the character of the descendants who have been spiritually influenced by a person's life.

HOMEBUILDERS PRINCIPLE #11:

The legacy you leave is determined by the life you live.

B. How to Leave a Legacy That Will Outlive You

According to 2 Timothy 2:2 and Psalm 78:3-8, you can leave spiritual as well as physical descendants.

1. Read Matthew 28:19,20. How do you leave a spiritual legacy?

     _____

2. According to Deuteronomy 6:4-9, how do you leave a godly legacy through your influence on your children, your physical descendants?

     _____

AN EXAMPLE OF LEAVING A SPIRITUAL LEGACY

As you near the completion of this study, you have become part of the godly legacy from a remarkable single woman who left no physical descendants. Humanly speaking, this study might never have been created if it had not been that Dr. Henrietta Mears befriended a young couple in the early years of their spiritual growth. Bill Bright, founder of Campus Crusade for Christ, and his wife Vonette were strongly influenced by Dr. Mears.

Many other individuals and organizations are part of the spiritual legacy left by Dr. Mears, including Billy Graham, Richard Halverson (former Chaplain of the United States Senate), Gospel Light Publications (a major producer of Bible study resources and Christian literature), Forest Home (one of the largest Christian conference centers in the United States), and Gospel Literature International (GLINT—a service organization aiding in the translation of Christian literature throughout the world).

If you have grown spiritually through this study, then you are a part of the spiritual legacy of Henrietta Mears. Do you believe that God could still be multiplying **your** spiritual legacy three generations from now?

HOMEBUILDERS PRINCIPLE #12:

Your marriage should leave a legacy of love that will influence future generations.

C. Thinking of My Legacy

1. What do you want your legacy to be?

     _____

2. What people do you need to influence for God?

     _____

3. What are some tasks in your church you are gifted to tackle?

     _____

4. What project should you support?

     _____

Make a Date

Make a date with your mate this week to complete the last **HomeBuilders Project**.

_____   _____   _____

Date   Time   Location

Recommended Reading

Staying Close by Dennis Rainey

"A Mother's Influence," "A Word to Dads," "Your Family Can Make the Difference," and "How to Become a HomeBuilder" are recommended chapters for this session.

Dream Big: The Henrietta Mears Story edited by Earl Roe.

Individually: 10-20 Minutes

Write out a description of the legacy you desire to leave...

    a.   to your physical descendants—your children, if God so blesses.

_____

    b.   to your spiritual descendants—those you lead to Christ and disciple.

_____

Interact as a Couple: 10-20 Minutes

1.   Compare your descriptions, then make one common description of the legacy you both desire to leave...

    a.   for your physical descendants.

_____

    b.   for your spiritual descendants.

_____

2.   Copy or type your statement and place it at work or home as a reminder of your objective. You may want to mount or frame it.

3.   Discuss options that are available to you (individually and as a couple) to equip and assist you to leave a godly legacy (local church, Bible study group, outreach event).

_____

4.   Write one major objective you wish to accomplish this year in helping you...

    a.   leave a godly line of physical descendants.

_____

    b.   leave a godly line of spiritual descendants.

_____

The Four Spiritual Laws*

Just as there are physical laws that govern the physical universe, so are there spiritual laws that govern your relationship with God.

Law One: God loves you and offers a wonderful plan for your life.

God's Love

"For God so loved the world, that He gave His only begotten Son, that whoever believes in Him should not perish, but have eternal life" (John 3:16).

God's Plan

(Christ speaking) "I came that they might have life, and might have it abundantly" (that it might be full and meaningful) (John 10:10).

Why is it that most people are not experiencing the abundant life? Because...

Law Two: Man is sinful and separated from God. Therefore, he cannot know and experience God's love and plan for his life.

Man Is Sinful

"For all have sinned and fall short of the glory of God" (Romans 3:23).

Man was created to have fellowship with God; but, because of his stubborn self-will, chose to go his own independent way, and fellowship with God was broken. This self-will, characterized by an attitude of active rebellion or passive indifference, is evidence of what the Bible calls sin.

Man Is Separated

"For the wages of sin is death" (spiritual separation from God) (Romans 6:23).

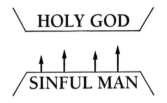

This diagram illustrates that God is holy and man is sinful. A great gulf separates the two. The arrows illustrate that man is continually trying to reach God and the abundant life through his own efforts, such as a good life, philosophy, or religion.

The third law explains the only way to bridge this gulf...

> ### Law Three: Jesus Christ is God's only provision for man's sin. Through Him you can know and experience God's love and plan for your life.

He Died in Our Place

"But God demonstrates His own love toward us, in that while we were yet sinners, Christ died for us" (Romans 5:8).

He Rose from the Dead

"Christ died for our sins . . . He was buried . . . He was raised on the third day according to the Scriptures . . . He appeared to [Peter], then to the twelve. After that He appeared to more than five hundred . . ." (1 Corinthians 15:3-6).

He Is the Only Way to God

"Jesus said to him, 'I am the way, and the truth, and the life; no one comes to the Father, but through Me'" (John 14:6).

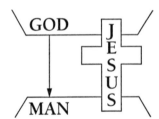

This diagram illustrates that God has bridged the gulf that separates us from Him by sending His Son, Jesus Christ, to die on the cross in our place to pay the penalty for our sins. It is not enough just to know these three laws...

> ### Law Four: We must individually receive Jesus Christ as Savior and Lord; then we can know and experience God's love and plan for our lives.

We Must Receive Christ

"But as many as received Him, to them He gave the right to become children of God, even to those who believe in His name" (John 1:12).

We Receive Christ Through Faith

"For by grace you have been saved through faith; and that not of yourselves, it is the gift of God; not as a result of works, that no one should boast" (Ephesians 2:8,9).

When We Receive Christ, We Experience a New Birth

(Read John 3:1-8.)

We Receive Christ by Personal Invitation

(Christ is speaking) "Behold, I stand at the door and knock; if any one hears My voice and opens the door, I will come in to him" (Revelation 3:20).

Receiving Christ involves turning to God from self (repentance) and trusting Christ to come into our lives to forgive our sins and to make us the kind of people He wants us to be. Just to agree intellectually that Jesus Christ is the Son of God and that He died on the cross for our sins is not enough. Nor is it enough to have an emotional experience. We receive Jesus Christ by faith, as an act of the will.

These two circles represent two kinds of lives:

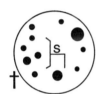

SELF-DIRECTED LIFE
S - Self is on the throne
† - Christ is outside of the life
• - Interests are directed by self, often resulting in discord and frustration

CHRIST-DIRECTED LIFE
† - Christ is in the life and on the throne
S - Self is yielding to Christ
• - Interests are directed by Christ, resulting in harmony with God's plan

Which circle best represents your life?

Which circle would you like to have represent your life?

The following explains how you can receive Christ:

You Can Receive Christ Right Now by Faith Through Prayer

(Prayer is talking with God.)

God knows your heart and is not so concerned with your words as He is with the attitude of your heart. The following is a suggested prayer:

> *Lord Jesus, I need You. Thank You for dying on the cross for my sins. I open the door of my life and receive You as my Savior and Lord. Thank You for forgiving my sins and giving me eternal life. Make me the kind of person You want me to be.*

Does this prayer express the desire of your heart?

If it does, pray this prayer right now, and Christ will come into your life, as He promised.

*Written by Bill Bright. Copyright © Campus Crusade for Christ, Inc., 1965. All rights reserved.

Have You Made the Wonderful Discovery of the Spirit-Filled Life?*

Every day can be an exciting adventure for the Christian who knows the reality of being filled with the Holy Spirit and who lives constantly, moment by moment, under His gracious control.

The Bible tells us that there are three kinds of people:

1. NATURAL MAN (one who has not received Christ)

"But a natural man does not accept the things of the Spirit of God; for they are foolishness to him, and he cannot understand them, because they are spiritually appraised" (1 Corinthians 2:14).

SELF-DIRECTED LIFE
S - Self is on the throne
† - Christ is outside of the life
• - Interests are directed by self, often resulting in discord and frustration

2. SPIRITUAL MAN (one who is controlled and empowered by the Holy Spirit)

"But he who is spiritual appraises all things..." (1 Corinthians 2:15).

CHRIST-DIRECTED LIFE
† - Christ is on the throne of the life
S - Ego or self is dethroned
• - Interests are under control of infinite God, resulting in harmony with God's plan

3. CARNAL MAN (one who has received Christ, but who lives in defeat because he trusts in his own efforts to live the Christian life)

SELF-DIRECTED LIFE
S - Ego or finite self is on the throne
† - Christ is dethroned
• - Interests controlled by self, often resulting in discord and frustration

"And I, brethren, could not speak to you as to spiritual men, but as to carnal men, as to babes in Christ. I gave you milk to drink, not solid food; for you were not yet able to receive it. Indeed, even now you are not yet able, for you are still carnal. For since there is jealousy and strife among you, are you not fleshly, and are you not walking like mere men?" (1 Corinthians 3:1-3).

A. God Has Provided for Us an Abundant and Fruitful Christian Life.

Jesus said, "I came that they might have life, and might have it abundantly" (John 10:10).

"I am the vine, you are the branches; he who abides in Me, and I in him, he bears much fruit; for apart from Me you can do nothing" (John 15:5).

"But the fruit of the Spirit is love, joy, peace, patience, kindness, goodness, faithfulness, gentleness, self-control; against such things there is no law" (Galatians 5:22,23).

"But you shall receive power when the Holy Spirit has come upon you; and you shall be My witnesses both in Jerusalem, and in all Judea and Samaria, and even to the remotest part of the earth" (Acts 1:8).

THE SPIRITUAL MAN

Some Personal Traits That Result from Trusting God:

Christ-centered		Love
Empowered by the Holy Spirit		Joy
Introduces others to Christ		Peace
Effective prayer life		Patience
Understands God's Word		Kindness
Trusts God		Goodness
Obeys God		Faithfulness

The degree to which these traits are manifested in the life depends upon the extent to which the Christian trusts the Lord with every detail of his, life, and upon his maturity in Christ. One who is only beginning to understand the ministry of the Holy

Spirit should not be discouraged if he is not as fruitful as more mature Christians who have known and experienced this truth for a longer period.

Why is it that most Christians are not experiencing the abundant life?

B. Carnal Christians Cannot Experience the Abundant and Fruitful Christian Life.

The carnal man trusts in his own efforts to live the Christian life:

1. He is either uninformed about, or has forgotten, God's love, forgiveness and power (Romans 5:8-10; Hebrews 10:1-25; 1 John 1; 2:1-3; 2 Peter 1:9; Acts 1:8).
2. He has an up-and-down spiritual experience.
3. He cannot understand himself—he wants to do what is right, but cannot.
4. He fails to draw upon the power of the Holy Spirit to live the Christian life.
    (1 Corinthians 3:1-3; Romans 7:15-24; 8:7; Galatians 5:16-18)

THE CARNAL MAN

Some or all of the following traits may characterize the Christian who does not fully trust God:

Ignorance of his spiritual heritage
Unbelief
Disobedience
Loss of love for God and for others
Poor prayer life
No desire for Bible study

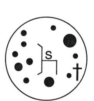

Legalistic attitude
Discouragement
Impure thoughts
Jealousy
Guilt
Critical Spirit
Worry
Frustration
Aimlessness

(The individual who professes to be a Christian but who continues to practice sin should realize that he may not be a Christian at all, according to 1 John 2:3; 3:6,9; Ephesians 5:5.)

The third truth gives us the only solution to this problem...

C. Jesus Promised the Abundant and Fruitful Life as the Result of Being Filled (Controlled and Empowered) by the Holy Spirit.

The Spirit-filled life is the Christ-controlled life by which Christ lives His life in and through us in the power of the Holy Spirit (John 15).

1. One becomes a Christian through the ministry of the Holy Spirit, according to John 3:1-8. From the moment of spiritual birth, the Christian is indwelt by the Holy Spirit at all times (John 1:12; Colossians 2:9,10; John 14:16,17). Though all Christians are indwelt by the Holy Spirit, not all Christians are filled (controlled and empowered) by the Holy Spirit.
2. The Holy Spirit is the source of the overflowing life (John 7:37-39).

3. The Holy Spirit came to glorify Christ (John 16:1-5). When one is filled with the Holy Spirit, he is a true disciple of Christ.

4. In His last command before His Ascension, Christ promised the power of the Holy Spirit to enable us to be witnesses for Him (Acts 1:1-9).

    How, then, can one be filled with the Holy Spirit?

D. We Are Filled (Controlled and Empowered) by the Holy Spirit by Faith; Then We Can Experience the Abundant and Fruitful Life that Christ Promised to Each Christian.

You can appropriate the filling of the Holy Spirit *right now* if you:

1. Sincerely desire to be controlled and empowered by the Holy Spirit (Matthew 5:6; John 7:37-39).

2. Confess your sins.

    By faith thank God that He has forgiven all of your sins—past, present, and future—because Christ died for you (Colossians 2:13-15; 1 John 1; 2:1-3; Hebrews 10:1-17).

3. By faith claim the fullness of the Holy Spirit, according to:

    a. HIS COMMAND—Be filled with the Spirit. "And do not get drunk with wine, for that is dissipation, but be filled with the Spirit" (Ephesians 5:18).

    b. HIS PROMISE—He will always answer when we pray according to His will. "And this is the confidence which we have before Him, that, if we ask anything according to His will, He hears us. And if we know that He hears us in whatever we ask, we know that we have the requests which we have asked from Him" (1 John 5:14,15).

Faith can be expressed through prayer...

How to Pray in Faith to Be Filled with the Holy Spirit

We are filled with the Holy Spirit by faith alone. However, true prayer is one way of expressing your faith. The following is a suggested prayer:

> *Dear Father, I need You. I acknowledge that I have been in control of my life; and that, as a result, I have sinned against You. I thank You that You have forgiven my sins through Christ's death on the cross for me. I now invite Christ to again take control of the throne of my life. Fill me with the Holy Spirit as You commanded me to be filled, and as You promised in your Word that You would do if I asked in faith. I pray this in the name of Jesus. As an expression of my faith, I now thank You for taking control of my life and for filling me with the Holy Spirit.*

Does this prayer express the desire of your heart? If so, bow in prayer and trust God to fill you with the Holy Spirit right now.

How to Know that You are Filled (Controlled and Empowered) by the Holy Spirit

Did you ask God to fill you with the Holy Spirit? Do you know that you are now filled with the Holy Spirit? On what authority? (On the trustworthiness of God Himself and His Word: Hebrews 11:6; Romans 14:22,23.)

Do not depend upon feelings. The promise of God's Word, not our feelings, is our authority. The Christian lives by faith (trust) in the trustworthiness of God Himself and His Word. This train diagram illustrates the relationship between **fact** (God and His Word), **faith** (our trust in God and His Word), and **feeling** (the result of our faith and obedience) (John 14:21).

The train will run with or without the caboose. However, it would be futile to attempt to pull the train by the caboose. In the same way, we, as Christians, do not depend upon feelings or emotions, but we place our faith (trust) in the trustworthiness of God and the promises of His Word.

How to Walk in the Spirit

Faith (trust in God and His promises) is the only means by which a Christian can live the Spirit-controlled life. As you continue to trust Christ moment by moment:

1. Your life will demonstrate more and more of the fruit of the Spirit (Galatians 5:22,23); and will be more and more conformed to the image of Christ (Romans 12:2; 2 Corinthians 3:18).
2. Your prayer life and study of God's Word will become more meaningful.
3. You will experience His power in witnessing (Acts 1:8).
4. You will be prepared for spiritual conflict against the world (1 John 2:15-17); against the flesh (Galatians 5:16,17); and against Satan (1 Peter 5:7-9; Ephesians 6:10-13).
5. You will experience His power to resist temptation and sin (1 Corinthians 10:13; Philippians 4:13; Ephesians 1:19-23; 6:10; 2 Timothy 1:7; Romans 6;1-16).

Spiritual Breathing

By faith you can continue to experience God's love and forgiveness.

If you become aware of an area of your life (an attitude or an action) that is displeasing to the Lord, even though you are walking with Him and sincerely desiring to serve Him, simply thank God that He has forgiven your sins—past, present and future—on the basis of Christ's death on the cross. Claim His love and forgiveness by faith and continue to have fellowship with Him.

If you retake the throne of your life through sin—a definite act of disobedience—breathe spiritually.

Spiritual Breathing (exhaling the impure and inhaling the pure) is an exercise in faith that enables you to continue to experience God's love and forgiveness.

1. Exhale—confess your sin—agree with God concerning your sin and thank Him for His forgiveness of it, according to 1 John 1:9 and Hebrews 10:1-25. Confession involves repentance—a change in attitude and action.

2. Inhale—surrender the control of your life to Christ, and appropriate (receive) the fullness of the Holy Spirit by faith. Trust that He now controls and empowers you, according to the *command* of Ephesians 5:18, and the promise of 1 John 5:14,15.

Be a HomeBuilder in Your Community.

You've just finished one of the most important construction projects in your life—helping couples grow closer to each other and to God. But the work doesn't stop when the foundation is laid. You can continue helping couples build a solid framework for their marriages by introducing them to **The HomeBuilders Couples Series**®. Hundreds of thousands of couples across the nation have already begun to build stronger marriages in **HomeBuilders** small groups. Even first-time group leaders can lead these studies at home, comfortably and with confidence. It's a fun way for couples to get closer to each other and to God—and a great way to get to know their neighbors.

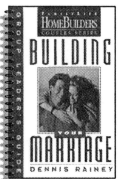

Building Your Marriage
By Dennis Rainey

Help couples get closer together than they ever imagined possible.

- Leader's Guide ISBN 08307.16130
- Study Guide ISBN 08307.16122

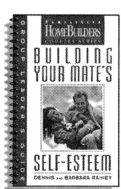

Building Your Mate's Self-Esteem
By Dennis & Barbara Rainey

Marriage is God's workshop for self-esteem.

- Leader's Guide ISBN 08307.16173
- Study Guide ISBN 08307.16165

Building Teamwork in Your Marriage
By Robert Lewis

Help couples celebrate and enjoy their differences.

- Leader's Guide ISBN 08307.16157
- Study Guide ISBN 08307.16149

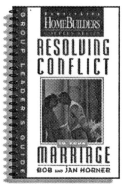

Resolving Conflict in Your Marriage
By Bob & Jan Horner

Turn conflict into love and understanding.

- Leader's Guide ISBN 08307.16203
- Study Guide ISBN 08307.16181

Mastering Money in Your Marriage
By Ron Blue

Put an end to conflicts and find out how to use money to glorify God.

- Leader's Guide ISBN 08307.16254
- Study Guide ISBN 08307.16246

Growing Together in Christ
By David Sunde

Discover how Christ is central to your marriage.

- Leader's Guide ISBN 08307.16297
- Study Guide ISBN 08307.16289

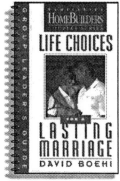

Life Choices for a Lasting Marriage
By David Boehi

Find out how to make the right choices in your marriage.

- Leader's Guide ISBN 08307.16262
- Study Guide ISBN 08307.16270

Managing Pressure in Your Marriage
By Dennis Rainey & Robert Lewis

Learn how obedience to God will take pressure off your marriage.

- Leader's Guide ISBN 08307.16319
- Study Guide ISBN 08307.16300

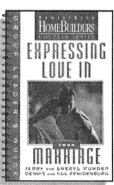

Expressing Love in Your Marriage
By Jerry & Sheryl Wunder and Dennis & Jill Eenigenburg

Discover God's plan for your love life by seeking God's best for your mate.

- Leader's Guide ISBN 08307.16661
- Study Guide ISBN 08307.16688

Tools for a Family Reformation

FAMILYLIFE CONFERENCES

FamilyLife Conferences are bringing meaningful, positive change to thousands of couples and families every year. The conferences, offered throughout the country, are based on solid biblical principles and are designed to provide couples and parents—in just one weekend—with the skills to build and enhance their marriages and families.

"A Weekend to Remember"

The FamilyLife Marriage Conference gives you the opportunity to slow down and focus on your spouse and your relationship. You will spend an insightful weekend together, doing fun couples' projects and hearing from dynamic speakers on real-life solutions for building and enhancing oneness in your marriage.

Take a Weekend to Raise Your Children for a Lifetime!

The FamilyLife Parenting Conference will equip you with the principles and tools you need to be more effective parents for a lifetime. Whether you're just getting started or in the turbulent years of adolescence, you'll learn biblical blueprints for raising your children.

To register or receive a free brochure and schedule for these conferences, call FamilyLife at 1-800-FL-TODAY.

"FamilyLife Today" Radio Program

Tune in to good news for families

More than 1,000,000 listeners across the nation are tuning in weekly to "FamilyLife Today," winner of the 1995 National Religious Broadcasters Radio Program Producer of the Year award. FamilyLife executive director Dennis Rainey and cohost Bob Lepine provide a fast-paced half hour of interviews and address the issues your family faces. So tune in this week and take advantage of this unique opportunity to be encouraged in your marriage and family.

Call 1-800-FL-TODAY for the times and stations near you.

Real FamilyLife Magazine

A new resource for building families

Our brand-new magazine, *Real FamilyLife,* is designed to communicate practical, biblical truth on marriage and family. Published eight times a year, each issue features articles, columns, and projects by Dennis and Barbara Rainey and others who will help you build a godly family.

To receive more information about FamilyLife resources, call 1-800-FL-TODAY.

FamilyLife Internet Site

Our site on the World Wide Web (www.familylife-ccc.org) gives people around the world access to our radio programming and materials. Visitors can listen to "FamilyLife Today" 24 hours a day, and they'll find a list of all radio stations carrying the program. In addition, they'll find the *Moments Together for Couples* daily devotional and a FamilyLife Marriage Conference online brochure with dates and locations for all conference sites in the United States.

FAMILYLIFE™

Bringing Timeless Principles Home

P.O. Box 23840
Little Rock, AR 72221-3840
(501)223-8663 ▪ 1-800-FL-TODAY
A division of Campus Crusade for Christ Incorporated